Anime, and the culture created by Japanese Animation, is of long-standing, and data about the subject fills the internet. All who wish to know more about the subject this book presents may find what they seek on the World Wide Web. Research over the past decades has placed my thinking in the middle of this phenomenon and as a professional teacher I have developed my own perspective. This means that I and others may come to the same or different conclusions on given aspects of animation. A wise King once said, "... there is no new thing under the sun." Consequently, in an effort to digest the mass of available material, I may have quoted some authors inadvertently.

All The World Is Anime

Religions, Myths & Spiritual Metaphors in the World of Japanimation & Manga

Isao Ebihara

an imprint of
GlobalEd AdvancePress

All The World is Anime
Copyright © 2010 by Isao Ebihara

Library of Congress Control Number: 2009942148

Ebihara, Isao., 1958 --
All The World is Anime
ISBN 978-1-935434-05-4

Subject Codes and Description:
1: LIT008030: Literature – Criticism: Asian-Japanese;
2:ART504000: Art-Animation; 3: HIS021000: History:Asian-Japan

All rights reserved, including the right to reproduce this book or any part thereof in any form, except for inclusion of brief quotations in a review, without the written permission of the author and GlobalEdAdvance Press.

Printed in the United States of America

Cover Anime Artist: David Sivertsen
All Rights Reserved
dave.longquan@gmail.com

The Press does not have ownership of the contents of a book; this is the author's work and the author owns the copyright. All theory, concepts, constructs, and perspectives are those of the author and not necessarily the Press. They are presented for open and free discussion of the issues involved. All comments and feedback should be directed to the Email: [comments4author@aol.com] and the comments will be forwarded to the author for response.

Published by
Post-Gutenberg Books™
An Imprint of
GlobalEdAdvancePress™
www.globaledadvance.org

Dedicated to my late mother

Ayako Ebihara

(1935 - 2007)

Table of Contents

Introduction
The Background of Otaku Culture
7

Chapter 2
World of Shinto & Animism by Hayao Miyazaki
(宮崎 駿)
17

Chapter 3
Space Operas & World of Fantasy by Leiji Matsumoto
(松本 零士)
75

Chapter 4
Dynamic Mythological World of Go Nagai
(永井 豪)
113

Chapter 5
Apocalyptic Mecha Action: Neon Genesis Evangelion
(新世紀エヴァンゲリオン, Shin Seiki Evangerion)
151

Chapter 6
Conclusion – Otaku Manifesto
179

1

Introduction

The Background of Otaku Culture

In today's North America, the term *Otaku* refers to those who are heavily into *anime,* or Japanese animation and *manga,* or Japanese comic books. All video stores carry some anime videos, and Chapters Book Stores all over the Lower Mainland have a large section for manga and sell various magazines specialized in anime and manga. According to Snow Wildsmith (2008), a librarian specialized in comics and teen fictions, anime and manga are important genres of graphic novels in North America. She also stated that many teen fictions and comics here are also based on the stories of Japanese anime and manga and she introduced some of them in her blog[1].

Etymology

Otaku (おたく or オタク, Otaku) is a derisive Japanese term used to refer to people with obsessive interests, particularly anime and manga. Otaku refers to someone who stays at home all the time and doesn't have a life (no social life, no love life, etc). Usually an otaku person has nothing better to do with their life, so they pass the time by watching anime, playing videogames and surfing the internet. Otaku is also used to refer to a nerd/geek/hacker/programmer.

---

1 The Only True Magic. http://myreadingproject.blogspot.com/ [accessed May 2008]

Otaku is derived from an honorific Japanese term for another's house or family (お宅, 御宅 otaku) that is also used as an honorific second-person pronoun (roughly equivalent to "usted" in Spanish). The modern slang form, which is distinguished from the older usage by being written only in hiragana (おたく) or katakana (オタク), or rarely in rōmaji, appeared in the 1980s. It appears to have been coined by the humorist and essayist Akio Nakamori in his 1983 series 'An Investigation of Otaku' (『おたく』の研究, "Otaku" no Kenkyū), printed in a magazine entitled Manga Burikko, that observed that this form of address was unusually common among geeks and nerds. It was apparently a reference to someone who communicates with their equals using (unnecessarily) the distant and formal pronoun, and spends most of their time at home.

The term was popularized in the English speaking world in William Gibson's 1996 novel Idoru, which has several references to otaku. In particular, the term was defined as 'pathological-techno-fetishist-with-social-deficit.' In an April 2001 edition of The Observer, William Gibson explained his view of the term:

The otaku, the passionate obsessive, the information age's embodiment of the "connoisseur," more concerned with the accumulation of data than of objects, seems a natural crossover figure in today's interface of British and Japanese cultures. I see it in the eyes of the Portobello dealers, and in the eyes of the Japanese collectors: a perfectly calm train-spotter frenzy, murderous and sublime. Understanding otaku-hood is one of the keys to understanding the culture of the web. There is something profoundly post-national about it, extra-geographic. We are all curators, in the post-modern world, whether we want to be or not (Gibson, 2001).

Summarizing his statement, Otaku prefer data to objects, are

The Background of Otaku Culture

post-national and extra-geographical. Otakuhood is a culture of Web, in which all are curators of personal museum (typically post-modern). They live in an age in which everyone lives in his or her own personal space with personal museum.

Another potential etymology for the term comes from the May 2006 issue of EX Taishuu magazine, which claims that use of the term started among the fanbase of the 1982 – 1983 TV series Super Dimension Fortress Macross, as the main character of the show had a habit of addressing others as "otaku", which fans started to emulate.

Another source for the term comes from the works of science fiction author Motoko Arai. In his book Wrong About Japan, Peter Carey interviews the novelist, artist and Gundam chronicler Yuka Minakawa. She reveals that Arai used the word in her novels as a second-person pronoun, and the readers adopted the term for themselves.

In Japan

In modern Japanese colloquialism, the term otaku refers to an overtly enthusiastic and obsessive fan, or is specialized in any one particular theme, topic, or hobby. Common uses are anime otaku (one who sometimes enjoys many days of excessive anime watching with no rest) and manga otaku (a fan of Japanese graphic novels), pasokon otaku (personal computer geeks), gēmu otaku (video game maniacs), and idol otaku that are extreme fans of idols, heavily promoted singing girls. There are also tetsudō otaku or denshamania (metrophiles) and gunji otaku or (military geeks). While these are the most common uses of otaku, the term can be applied to anything like (music otaku, martial arts otaku, cooking otaku, etc).

The loan-word from the West maniakku or mania (from the

English "maniac" and "mania") is often used in relation to special interests and favorite activities. It can indicate someone with otaku inclinations, (for example - Gundam Mania would describe a person who is extremely into the anime series Gundam). It can also describe the focus of such interests (a maniakku ge-mu would be a particularly underground and illegally made game appealing primarily to otaku). The nuance of maniakku in Japanese is softer and less likely to cause offense than otaku.

Some of Japan's otaku use the term humorously to describe themselves and their friends, accepting their position as obsessive mania, however, some even use the term proudly, attempting to reclaim it from its negative connotations. In general colloquial usage however, most Japanese prefer not to be described in a serious fashion as "otaku", many even consider it to be a serious insult.

Although stereotypically male, there are also many female otaku called "fujoshi." A small alleyway of Tokyo's Higashi Ikebukuro district is known as "Otome Road" ("Maiden's road"). An interesting modern look into the otaku culture has surfaced with an allegedly true story surfacing on the largest internet bulletin board 2channel: "Densha Otoko" or "Train Man", a love story about an otaku man and a beautiful woman who meet on a train. The story has enjoyed a compilation in novel form, several comic book adaptations, a movie released in June 2005, a theme song Love Parade for this movie by a popular Japanese band named Orange Range and a television series that aired on Fuji TV from June to September 2005. The drama has become a hot topic in Japan, and the novel, film and television series give a closer look into the otaku culture. In Japan its popularity and positive portrayal of the main character has helped to reduce negative stereotypes about otaku, and increase the acceptability of some otaku interests and activities. Perhaps encouraged by this reduction

The Background of Otaku Culture

in stigma, a few famous Japanese celebrities, actors and models have come out about their otaku hobbies.

A subset of otaku are the *Akiba-kei*, men who spend a great deal of time in Akihabara in Tokyo and who are mainly obsessive about anime, manga and games. Sometimes the term is used to describe something pertaining to the subculture that surrounds anime characters and games in Japan. This subculture places an emphasis on certain services and has its own system for judgment of anime, dating simulations and/or role-playing games and some manga based upon the level of fan service in the work. Another popular criterion about ideal female protagonists of the show is based upon a level of stylized cuteness and child-like behavior. In addition, this subculture places great emphasis on knowledge of individual key animators and directors and of minute details within works. The international otaku subculture is developed from the Japanese one, but differs in many areas often based upon region.

In English/Internationally

The term otaku in English is relatively new and a loanword from the Japanese language. In English, it is used to refer specifically to a fan of anime and/or manga, though it can sometimes refer to any kind of "geek". It also is used to refer to people who appear to be obsessed with Japan and its culture in a broader sense. The term serves as a label not unlike Trekkie or fanboy. However, use of the label can be a source of contention among some anime fans in the West, particularly those who are aware of the negative connotations the term has in Japan. Unpleasant stereotypes about otaku prevail in worldwide fan communities, and some anime fans outside of Japan express concern about the effect these more extreme fans can have on the reputation of their interests (not unlike sentiments in the comic book and science fiction fandoms).

It should be noted that the English term geek is not a precise translation of the Japanese otaku. The term *otaku* came into existence as a significantly greater negative connotation than *geek* did in the West, although geek also started as a derogatory. The term otaku in Japanese used to have suggested a creepy, obsessive loner who rarely leaves the house. In English, geek can possibly suggest a person who may be socially awkward but who is also intelligent and may be fairly "normal" aside from their interest in certain typically 'geekish' pursuits (video games, comic books, computers, etc.). Otaku is closer in connotation to the English nerd, but the closest English-language analogue to otaku is probably the British English term anorak. Both of these English-language terms have more emphatically negative connotations of poor social skills and obsessive interest in a topic that seems strange or boring to others.

While otaku in English-speaking contexts is generally understood to mean geek or even fan, this usage is not widely known in Japan. Casual use of this term may confuse or offend native Japanese speakers.

Otaku Sub-culture Today

According to Thomas Lamarre (2006), those from Otaku sub-culture have different focus or attentions from the general public as they view animations. As Otaku compulsively replay videos of such favourite series as Macross, they began to perceive differences in animation styles within and between episodes. The result was a new attention to what might be considered flaws, inconsistencies or trivial details by other viewers. Lamarre maintains that, for the otaku, however, these apparently insignificant details become part of the viewing experience, making the experience of viewing akin to scanning for information, rather than reading a story (whence perhaps Azuma's thoughts about the end of narrative structures and the rise of database structures). In effect, what was peripheral becomes central; or rather there is a breakdown in the visual ordering of central and peripheral that results in a non-hierarchical visual field of information. Otaku viewers abandoned a typical modernistic interpretation of the discourse to follow the story line in a linear fashion and dare to use Post-Modernist method of understanding the discourse.

According to Toshio Okada, the founder of Gainax Studios (1996), "true" anime viewers (otaku) devote as much attention to the work of character designers and animators as to directors, producers or writers. Okada argues, for instance, that anime series are the work of many different creators, and so there is no single story. This follows from Okada's discussion of the otaku fan's attention to inconsistencies as a new aesthetic and new form of reception—what might appear as stylistic inconsistency to non-otaku viewers appears to the otaku as a dense aggregate of the works of a series of artists or producers, from which emerges a cooperative system. In brief, production is as distributive as vision.

Otaku & Techno-Orientalism

Toshiya Ueno (1996) maintains that Otaku Culture in the West produced a phenomena called Techno-Orientalism. Like the concept of "Orient," Techno-Orientalism, according to Ueno, is a fantasy about Asia (the vast majority of the Eurasian continent that is classified as non-West), created by the Westerners. He argues that the Orient exists in so far as the West needs it, because it brings the project of the West into focus. Naoki Sakai says on this point,

"The Orient does not connote any internal commonality among the names subsumed under it; it ranges from region in the Middle East to those in the Far East. One can hardly find anything religious, linguistic or cultural that is common among these varied areas. The Orient is neither a cultural, religious or linguistic unity. The principle of its identity lies outside itself: what endows it with some vague sense of unity is that Orient is that which is excluded and objectified by the West, in the service of its historical progress. From the outset the Orient is a shadow of the West."

Kumiko Sato (2007) also contends that the idea of techno-Orientalism best explicates the trend in associating Japaneseness with technology – now the West's fear of the Orient went hand in hand with the fear of high technology. The application of "cyborg philosophy" to Japan actually meant rephrasing the same cultural condition in a new language of technology. The cyborgian philosophy transforms humans into transgressive beings on the metaphysical level, thereby providing us with the deconstructionist illusion of decolorization and desexualization.

Sato quotes that Toshiya Ueno's 'Japanimation and Techno-Orientalism' (1996) further argued that anime that adopts Asian settings from American cyberpunk "reproduces a Japan" imaginarily separated from both West and East' by appropriating the Otherness of Asian automatons. In other words, Ueno and Sato views that Western Otaku identifies the fantasy world created by animation artists as "Orient" or imaginary Asia created by pre-modern Europeans. He continues that if the West invented the Orient, then the Techno-Orient also was invented by the world of information capitalism. In "Techno-Orientalism", Japan not only is located geographically, but also is projected chronologically. For Western Otaku, Japan has been located in the future of technology. Otaku see Japan as the future with Postmodernity, and it is a future that seems to be transcending and displacing Western modernity."

The Background of Otaku Culture

Here, I want to raise a question. What are some essential matters and philosophical assumptions behind the *anime* which might serve as the foundations of an entirely new trend and culture among the youth and young adults world-wide? In this book, I am going to introduce popular narratives by several well known *anime* and *manga* authors and discuss the religions, myths, archetypes and spiritual metaphors as well as the essentials of *Otakudom* behind these stories.

[2]Ishimori Production. Otaku USA. Herndon: VA, April 2009.[3]

---

2 ©2008 Ishimori Productions Inc, Toei Company Ltd. Adness Entertainment Co., Ltd.
3 The picture is used under "fair dealing" (Canada) and "fair use" (USA) provisions in copyright law.

2

World of Shinto & Animism by Hayao Miyazaki
(宮崎 駿)

Hayao Miyazaki (b.1941 in Tokyo) is the prominent director of many popular animated feature films. He is also known as the co-founder of Studio Ghibli, an animation studio and production company. He remained largely unknown to the West, outside of animation communities, until *Miramax Films* released his *Princess Mononoke* (1997). By that time, his films had already enjoyed both commercial and critical success in Japan and East Asia. Miyazaki's *Spirited Away* (2001) is the highest-grossing film of all time in Japan and also became the first anime film to win an Academy Award; Princess Mononoke had also briefly retained that distinction.[4]

Miyazaki's films often incorporate common themes, such as humanity's relationship to technology, nature and the spiritual world, and the difficulty of maintaining a pacifist ethic. The protagonists of his films are often strong, independent girls or young women, and the villains, if present, are often morally ambiguous characters with redeemable qualities.

---
4 Wikepedia: Hayao Miyazaki. Was available March 2008: http://en.wikipedia.org/wiki/Hayao_Miyazaki

Overall Miyazaki's films have been financially successful, and this success has led many movie critics to compare him with American animator Walt Disney. However, Miyazaki does not intend to build an animation empire, but sees himself as a fortunate animator with opportunities to utilize his talent and complete creative control. In 2006, Time Magazine voted Miyazaki one of the most influential Asians of the past 60 years.

Anime directed by Miyazaki that have won *the Animage Anime Grand Prix Award* include *Nausicaä of the Valley of the Wind* in 1984, *Castle in the Sky* in 1986, *My Neighbor Totoro* in 1988, and *Kiki's Delivery Service* in 1989.

Biography

Miyazaki, the second among four brothers, was born in Akebono-cho, in Bunkyō-ku, Tokyo. During the Second World War, Miyazaki's father Katsuji was director of Miyazaki Airplane, owned by his brother and Hayao's uncle, that made rudders for *Zero fighters*. During this time, Miyazaki drew airplanes and developed a lifelong fascination with aviation, later manifested as a recurring theme in his films and manga.

Miyazaki's mother was an avid reader with critical thinking who often questioned conventional ways of thinking and socially accepted norms. Miyazaki later said that he inherited his critical and skeptical thought from his mother. She underwent treatment for spinal tuberculosis from 1947 until 1955, and so the family had to move frequently. Miyazaki's film My Neighbor Totoro might be a reflection of his own experience during that period and features a family whose mother is afflicted.

During his high school year, Miyazaki saw the film *Hakujaden* or "The Tale of the White Serpent", which has been described as "the first-ever Japanese feature length color anime," and inspired him to start a career as an animator. However, in order to become an animator, he had to undergo extensive training and discipline to draw the human figure, since his prior work had been limited to airplanes and battleships. After high school, Miyazaki attended Gakushuin University, and graduated in 1963 with degrees in political science and economics. During his college years, Miyazaki was a member of the "Children's Literature research club," the "closest thing to a comics club in those days."

In April 1963, Miyazaki got a job at Toei Animation, working as an in-between artist on the anime Watchdog Bow Wow (Wanwan Chushingura). He was a leader in a labor dispute soon after his arrival, becoming chief secretary of Toei's labor union in 1964.

In October 1965, he married fellow animator Akemi Ota, who later left work to raise their two sons, Gorō and Keisuke. Gorō is now an animator and filmmaker, and has directed *Tales from Earthsea at Studio Ghibli*. Keisuke is a wood artist who has created pieces for the Ghibli Museum and who made the wood engraving shown in the Studio Ghibli film *Whisper of the Heart*.

Films

Miyazaki first gained recognition as an artist while working in a team on the Toei production *Gulliver's Travels Beyond the Moon* (1965). He found the original ending to the script unsatisfactory, and added his own idea, which became the ending used in the final film.

He later played an important role as chief animator, concept artist, and scene designer on *Hols: Prince of the Sun* (1968), a landmark animated film directed by Isao Takahata (born, 1935), with whom he continued to collaborate for the next three decades. Miyazaki played a crucial role in several movies like *Kimio Yabuki's Puss in Boots* (1969); *Flying Phantom Ship* (1969); *Animal Treasure Island and Ali Baba and the 40 Thieves* (1971).

Miyazaki left Toei in 1971 and joined A Pro, where he co-directed six episodes of the first *Lupin III* series with Isao Takahata. He and Takahata then began pre-production on a *Pippi Longstocking* series and drew extensive story boards for it. However, after traveling to Sweden to conduct research for the film and meet the original author, Astrid Lindgren, they were denied permission to complete the project, and it was canceled.

Instead of Pippi Longstocking, Miyazaki conceived, wrote, designed, and animated two *Panda! Go, Panda!* stories, which were directed by Takahata. Miyazaki's first film as a director was *The Castle of Cagliostro* (1979), a *Lupin III* adventure film.

Miyazaki's next film, *Nausicaä of the Valley of the Wind* (Kaze no Tani no Naushika, 1984), was a science fiction film that introduced many themes which recur in later films: a concern with ecology, a fascination with aircraft, and morally ambiguous characterizations, especially among villains. This was the first film both written and directed by Miyazaki. He adapted it from his manga series of the same title, which he began writing and illustrating two years earlier, but which remained incomplete until after the film's release.

Following the success of *Nausicaä of the Valley of the Wind*, Miyazaki co-founded the animation production company *Studio Ghibli* with Takahata in 1985, and has produced nearly all of his subsequent work through it.

Miyazaki continued to gain international recognition with his next three films which is characterized by his fascination with aviation. *Laputa: Castle in the Sky* (1986) recounts the adventure of two orphans seeking a magical floating island; *My Neighbor Totoro* (Tonari no Totoro, 1988) tells of the adventure of two girls in the early 1960s and their interaction with forest spirits; and *Kiki's Delivery Service* (1989), adapted from a novel by Eiko Kadono, tells the story of a small-town girl who leaves home to begin life as a witch in a big city.

Porco Rosso (1992) was a notable departure for Miyazaki, in that the main character was an adult male, an anti-fascist aviator transformed into a being that's part man, part pig. The film is set in 1920s Italy during during the First World War era and the main character is a bounty hunter who fights air pirates and an American soldier of fortune. The theme that the film explores is the tension between selfishness and duty. The film can also be viewed as an abstract self-portrait of the director; its subtext can be read as a fictionalized autobiography. Miyazaki himself held a political left-wing, anti-war and anti-fascist stance from his youth. He was almost always critical to the ruling conservative Liberal Democrat government during all his life.

Princess Mononoke (Mononoke Hime) in 1997 returns to the ecological and political themes of *Nausicaä of the Valley of the Wind*. The plot centers on the tension between the animal spirits who dwell in the forest and the humans who exploit the forest for industry. The film was a huge commercial success in Japan, where it became the highest grossing film of all time, until the later success of Titanic, and it ultimately won Best Picture at the Japanese Academy Awards. Miyazaki retired once after completing *Princess Mononoke*.

However, while on an extended vacation, Miyazaki spent time with the daughters of a friend, one of whom became his inspiration for his next movie Spirited Away (Sen to Chihiro no Kamikakushi, 2001) and the model of the main character Chihiro. Spirited Away is the story of a girl, drawn into a bizarre spirit world who works in a bathhouse for spiritual beings after her parents are turned into pigs by the sorceress who owns it. Released in Japan in July 2001, the film was Miyazaki's greatest success breaking attendance and box office records with ¥30.4 billion (approximately $300 million) in total gross earnings from more than 23 million viewings. It has received many awards, including Best Picture at the 2001 Japanese Academy Awards, Golden Bear (First Prize) at the 2002 Berlin Film Festival, and the 2002 Academy Award for Best Animated Feature.

Miyazaki completed production on *Howl's Moving Castle*, a film adaptation of a fantasy novel by Diana Wynne Jones (b 1934). Miyazaki came out of retirement following the sudden departure of original director Mamoru Hosoda. The film premiered at the 2004 Venice International Film Festival and won the Golden Osella award for animation technology. On November 20, 2004, *Howl's Moving Castle* opened to general audiences in Japan where it earned ¥1.4 billion in its first two days. The English language version was later released in the US by Walt Disney. In 2005, Miyazaki was awarded for lifetime achievement at the Venice Film Festival.

In 2006, *Nausicaä.net* reported Hayao Miyazaki's plans to direct a new film, rumored to be set in Kobe. Among areas Miyazaki's team visited during pre-production were an old café run by an elderly couple, and the view of a city from high in the mountains. The exact location of these places is censored from Studio Ghibli's production diaries. The studio has also announced that Miyazaki has begun creating storyboards for the film and that they are being produced in watercolor because the film will have an "unusual visual style." Studio Ghibli anticipates a production time of 20 months, with release slated for summer 2008.

In 2007, the film's title was announced as *Gake no ue no Ponyo*, translated into *"Ponyo on a Cliff."* The story is said to revolve around a five-year old boy, Sosuke, and Ponyo a piscus the Princess, who wants to become human. Studio Ghibli President Toshio Suzuki noted that "70 to 80 percent of the film takes place at sea." The movie was released in the summer 2008.

Manga

Miyazaki has written several manga, beginning in 1969 with his own version of a Western fairy tale *Puss in Boots* (Nagakutsu wo Haita Neko), which eventually became anime. His most significant work in this format is the seven-volume manga version of his tale *Nausicaä of the Valley of the Wind*, which he created from 1982 to 1994 and sold millions of copies worldwide. Another significant manga work is *A Trip to Tynemouth*, which was published in Japan in October 2006. Miyazaki based it on the young adult short stories of Robert Westall (1929 – 1993), a proliferate writer for both children and adults who grew up in England during the Second World War era. Few other memorable works are *Sabaku no Tami* (砂漠の民, People of the Desert), *Shuna no Tabi* (シュナの旅, The Journey of Shuna), *The Notebook of Various Images* (雑想ノート, Zassō Nōto), and *The Age of the Flying Boat*, which was the basis of his film *Porco Rosso*.

Underlined Themes & Motifs

Good & Evil

Most of Miyazaki's characters are dynamic, capable of change, and not easily caricatured into traditional good-evil dichotomies. Many menacing characters have redeemable features, and are not firmly defined as antagonists. Lady Eboshi of Princess Mononoke knowingly exploits the forests for raw materials at the expense of animal life, while simultaneously sheltering lepers and former prostitutes in her Tataraba or the city of iron. The film culminates in reconciliatory climax and conclusion, rather than the vanquishing of some irredeemable evil.

The same is true for *Spirited Away*, where, according to Miyazaki, "Chihiro the heroine is thrown into a strange world where the good and bad dwell together. She manages the life there not because she has destroyed the "evil," but because she has acquired the ability to survive." Some of Miyazaki's early films featured distinctly evil villains, as in *Castle of Cagliostro* or *Castle in the Sky*. Other films such as in *Kiki's Delivery Service* and *My Neighbor Totoro* are remarkable for having no villains at all. Some of these works have a strong flavor of traditional Japanese culture and ancient animistic spiritual beliefs.

Environmentalism & Anti-war

Miyazaki's films often emphasize environmentalism and the fragile nature of the Earth. In *My Neighbor Totoro*, the great tree tops a hillside on which magical creatures named Totoro reside, and the family worships this tree as a part of the Shinto rituals. This ecological consciousness is projected in *Princess Mononoke* with the giant primordial forest, complete with gigantic dragonflies, trees, flowers and wolves. In *Spirited Away*, Miyazaki environmentalism is made concrete through the "stink god" — a river spirit whose river, and consequently himself, has been polluted and so comes to the spiritual bath house and is cleansed by Chihiro the heroine.

In those three works, the author presents the narratives that the ecological well-being is jeopardized by military men and violent state-controlled armies. In each film, the conflict between the natural way of life and the military leaders with de facto power, and the land and resources is central to the plight of the protagonists. When battle scenes are shown in each, the militaristic music and ecological destruction is paramount to the endangerment of the inhabitants of the villages.

Both *Nausicäa* and *Princess Mononoke* feature strong anti-war sentiment. Ending the humans' hateful war with themselves and nature becomes the driving force of Ashitaka in *Princess Mononoke*. In the manga version of *Nausicaä*, Miyazaki spends much time depicting the brutality and suffering of war in graphic detail through most of the story. The post-apocalyptic world is filled with remains of the old civilizations that ended with wars and the destruction of the environment.

For Miyazaki, flying is a part of escapist fantasy from the ugly reality in which military leaders dominate the earth and her ecology and the environment is brutally mutilated. In addition to the many aerial devices and drawings of *Laputa: Castle in the Sky*, which is a flying city, the aviation theme is found in Nausicaä piloting her Mehve and the airborne armies in *Nausicaä of the Valley of the Wind*; Kiki riding her broomstick and watching dirigibles fly over her city in *Kiki's Delivery Service*; the large Totoro carrying Satsuki and Mei across the night sky in My Neighbor Totoro; Chihiro being borne by Haku in his dragon form in *Spirited Away* and Howl and Sophie soaring above their town in Howl's Moving Castle. In *Porco Rosso*, the protagonist flies to a remote island to escape his duties as well.

Politics

The influence of Miyazaki's early interest in Marxism and the conservationism that developed from it is apparent in some of his films, such as *Porco Rosso*. In *Castle in the Sky*, the working class is portrayed in idealized terms. However, Miyazaki claims to have abandoned Marxism while creating his manga *Nausicaa of the Valley of Wind*.

Influences

It is believed that a number of Western authors played influential roles in Miyazaki's work, including Ursula K. Le Guin (b. 1929), Lewis Carroll (1832 –1898), and Diana Wynne Jones (b. 1934). Miyazaki confided to Le Guin that her *Earthsea* has been a great influence on all his works, and that he has kept her books at his bedside.

Miyazaki and French writer and illustrator Jean Giraud (b. 1938) have influenced each other and have become friends as a result of their mutual admiration. *Monnaie de Paris* in France held an exhibition of their work titled *Miyazaki et Moebius: Deux Artistes Dont Les Dessins Prennent Vie* (Two Artists's Drawings Taking on a Life of Their Own) from December 2004 to April 2005. Both artists attended the opening of the exhibition. Also, Moebius has named his daughter Nausicaa after Miyazaki's heroine.

Miyazaki has been deeply influenced by another French writer and aviator, Antoine de Saint-Exupéry (1900—1944). He illustrated the Japanese covers of *Saint-Exupéry's Night Flight and Wind, Sand and Stars*, and wrote an afterword for Wind, Sand and Stars. Miyazaki's fascination with flying might be at least partly coming from the inspiration of Saint-Exupéry.

Additionally, in an interview broadcast on BBC Choice on 2002, Miyazaki cited the British authors Eleanor Farjeon (1881 – 1965), Rosemary Sutcliff (1920 - 1992), and Philippa Pearce (1920 -- 2006) as those who have greatly inspired his work. The filmmaker has also publicly expressed fondness for Ronald Dahl's (1916 – 1990) stories about pilots and airplanes; the image in *Porco Rosso* of a cloud of dead pilots was inspired by Dahl's *They Shall Not Grow Old*. Miyazaki seemed to have extracted the essences that these

Western authors created, in which characters have complex, and often ambiguous, motivations and incorporated them with elements of Japanese history and mythology in his work, such as My *Neighbor Totoro*, *Princess Mononoke*, and *Spirited Away*.

Shinto Motif

Many films made by Miyazaki including *Spirited Away* and *Princess Mononoke* contain many folk and Shrine Shinto motifs, either overtly or covertly. For instance, *Spirited Away* has an overt, explicit and visible theme based on Shinto mythology and religiousity.

Miyazaki often conveys positive, timely and sociologically relevant messages that support environmental conservation and are expressed through pagan spirituality and Shinto ideals of respect for nature. Shinto as a religion is not widely practiced in Western culture and can be considered a rich spirituality of which Westerners are not informed (Ono, 1962).[5] Miyazaki therefore grounds Shinto imagery and messages in archetypes, which are far more accessible globally and therefore, can cross the cultural divide between Western and Eastern contemporary society. This is evident in the popularity of Miyazaki's feature animations, which have greater, mainstream audiences in western society than any other Japanese feature animations. The messages of Miyazaki, in a pagan archetypal framework, were successfully universalized, became accessible to both Western and Eastern audiences. They are the vectors by which Miyazaki transmits his discourse to a greater, world-wide audience.

The presence of archetypes within Miyazaki's films and his ability to make relevant characters and narrative creates far more accessibility to the global audience because of

---
5 Sokyo Ono. Shinto --- The Kami Way (Rutland, Vermont, USA & Tokyo, Japan: Charles E. Tuttle company, 1962/1969)

their universality than Shinto practice. These archetypes are grounded in Shinto imagery, but remain relevant in today's society where the growing tradition of paganism and interest in archetypes – many of which derive from pagan systems of belief – facilitates a re-connection with ecosystems around them, as pagans attempt to understand ecosystems and environment in order to better live in harmony with it (Burnett, 1991)[6]. For this reason, these archetypes coming from Shinto and a wider range of paganism from various regions of the planet, are sending a message about our connection with the world around us as well as our self understanding within the ecological system.

Expanding upon the definitions of folk Shinto, in which the spiritual context of Miyazaki's films are placed in the light of the Jungian concept of archetypes, we may focus the analysis of archetypes on the following films; Princess Mononoke (1997), Nausicaä of the Valley of the Wind (1984) and Spirited Away (2001). Examining each film's narrative carefully, we may observe the following archetypes; Shamaness, Chaste Heroine, Animist Warrior, Greedy Magna Mater, Benevolent Kami and Impartial Kami and describe what elements constitute each one. In order to understand the archetypes, we must first understand paganism and Miyazaki's connection to the Shinto faith.

The terms paganism and neo-paganism are terms that encompass a wide range of spiritualities and cultures. On a fundamental level, all forms of paganism are 'nature religions.' They involve a re-orientation towards, and a 're-sacralisation of, both external nature and our own physical embodiment' (Pearson, 1998).[7] One aspect Shinto and paganism both

---

6   D Burnett. Dawning of the Pagan Moon: An Investigation into the Rise of Western Paganism. East Sussex: MARC, 1991.
7   J Pearson. Roberts, R. H. & Samuel, G. Introduction. In J. Pearson, R. H. Roberts & G. Samuel. (eds.). Nature Religion Today: Paganism in the Modern World. Edinburgh: Edinburgh University Press, 1998. (pp. 1-7).

share is 'the way in which man, gods and nature are closely interrelated on the same plane' (Earhart, 1974).[8] It is a tradition of immanent rather than transcendent spirituality.

Immanence is the presence of divinity or sacredness in the world around us. It is a particular feature of growing pagan, indigenous, pantheistic and animist spiritualities. Transcendence is the positioning of God and sacredness outside of our immediate world and is common to Christianity and Judaism. Transcendent paths are more common in western culture, where Christianity pervades much of our conditioning and awareness. Critics of Judeo-Christian tradition often consider that transcendent spirituality is directly responsible for a loss of pagan ideals and an increased degradation of nature (Roberts, 1998).[9] From the early Christian era, pagan themes have at times been considered subversive in western culture, and paganism is suppressed amongst some of the traditional forms of Christianity.

Hayao Miyazaki has acknowledged repeatedly – in interviews and elsewhere – his respect for, and indebtedness to, the tradition of Shinto (Boyd & Nishimura, 2004).[10] Most of his animations convey a Shinto perspective through characters and themes. There are different forms of Shinto, Miyazaki is a practitioner of folk Shinto, a less regimented form which is passed down from generation to generation (Ono, 1962). It is important to understand Shinto, as it informs Miyazaki's work, themes, plots, settings and characters. Shinto is a nature

---

[8] H. B. Earhart. The Religious Life of Man: Religion in the Japanese Experience; Sources and Interpretations (California: Dickenson Publishing Company, 1974).

[9] R. Roberts. The Cthonic Imperative: Gender, Religion and the Battle for the Earth. In J. Pearson, R. H. Roberts & G. Samuel. (eds.). Nature Religion Today: Paganism in the Modern World. Edinburgh: Edinburgh University Press, 1998. (pp. 57-73).

[10] J. W. Boyd & Nishimura, T. (2004b). Shinto Perspectives in Miyazaki's Anime Film 'Spirited Away' Footnotes. The Journal of Religion and Film. 8 (2). Retrieved September 8, 2005, from http://avalon.unomaha.edu/jrf/Vol8No2/Notes/BoydGroupNotes.htm

tradition, and a form of traditionalist paganism (Earhart, 1974; Tucker, 2003).[11] Shinto is an animist tradition that upholds a veneration and respect for kami, which are immanent and inherent in the world around us. Kami can be understood as that which is 'sacred' or 'godly' (Earhart, 1974). Kami includes, but is not limited to: Objects or phenomena designated from ancient times...qualities of growth, fertility and production; natural phenomena, such as wind and thunder; natural objects, such as the sun, mountains, rivers, trees and rocks; some animals; and ancestral spirits. (Ono, 1962).

Ono also notes that Shinto has no canon, all tradition is transmitted orally. Summerizing his statements, Shinto has no concept of original sin, it supports the idea that all people are born inherently good, in a similarly good world. Evil 'cannot originate in man or in this world, but comes from without'. If a person lives righteously; respecting the nature and tradition, descendents and the kami around them, they will lead a good life that is harmonious with all life around them. Folk Shinto – the most popular form of Shinto – is 'deeply rooted in the everyday life of the people'. Shinto is understood to be a form of paganism which is thought to 'bring one closer to an identity with nature' (Burnett, 1991).

Miyazaki & Moto-ori Norinaga

The core ideas that inform our understanding of "natural" Shinto were developed by Moto-ori Norinaga (1730-1801) in the Tokugawa period. A student of Kamo no Mabuchi (1697-1769) another prominent Japanese scholar of Edo period, Norinaga argued for a return to the idyllic simplicity of ancient Japan and the removal of foreign elements from Japanese culture. Through extensive studies of the Kojiki, a book that

---

11   J. A. Tucker. Anime and Historical Inversion in Miyazaki Hayao's 'Princess Mononoke.' Japanese Studies Review: A Publication of the Southern Japan Seminar & Florida International University 7, 2003. Retrieved September 8, 2005, from http://www.fiu.edu/~asian/jsr/Table%20of%20Cont%202003.pdf.

is sometimes described as the holy book of Shinto, Norinaga developed his thesis that in the remote past, Japanese people possessed a "kami-given nature" that allowed them to live in perfect harmony with their natural surroundings. Part of the success of his teachings stemmed from the emotionality of his appeal and the sense of nostalgia he invoked. Jun'ichi Isomae (2000) suggests that Norinaga's "affective" approach and conflation of the natural and the divine "laid the basis for the emotional debates on the nature of the heroic age that repeatedly played out during the postwar era."[12] Before Norinaga, Japanese history had mainly been taken from the Nihon shoki, 'Chronicle of Japan', written in 720 C.E. in Chinese. The Kojiki (literally 'Record of Ancient Things') was completed in 712 C.E. under the supervision of the imperial Yamato court, and details the creation myths of Izanagi and Izanami and events in "the age of the kami," including how the grandson of Amaterasu Omikami, Emperor Jimmu, was set upon the imperial throne.

In these ancient times, naturally occurring, awe-inspiring phenomena were given the title of kami, or gods, and were explained supernaturally. Around the time these beliefs arose, during the early Jomon (10,000 B.C.E.-300 B.C.E) and Yayoi periods (300 B.C.E.-300 C.E.), it was believed that respect for kami as divine beings was inseparably a part of the people's love of nature. Norinaga describes kami as:

The deities of heaven and earth that appear in the ancient texts and also the spirits enshrined in the shrines; furthermore, among all kinds of beings - including not only human beings but also such objects as birds, beasts, trees, grass, seas, mountains, and so forth - any being whatsoever which possesses some eminent quality out of the ordinary, and is awe-inspiring, is called kami. Eminence here does not refer

---
12 Jun 'Ichi Isomae. "Reappropriating the Japanese Myths: Moto-ori Norinaga and the Creation Myths of the Kojiki and Nihon Shoki," Japanese Journal of Religious Studies, l. 27,1-2, 2000.

simply to superiority in nobility, goodness, or meritoriousness. Evil or queer things, if they are extraordinarily awe-inspiring, are also called kami (Kojiki-den or Commentaries on the Kojiki, – 1764).[13]

Norinaga continues that the written character for kami, another way of reading the Chinese character for shin, can be literally translated as "above" which gives rise to the interpretation of "god" or "deity." Yet kami are not omniscient and transcendent in the Christian or Muslim sense, but exist in a similar way to the Greek gods: capable of human emotion and accessible to mortal communication. There was a sense of familiarity and friendliness between humans and kami; the kami were respected and honoured, but usually not feared.

Representations of kami and the natural world in Miyazaki's films express an underlying belief of the early Shinto worldview and theme, dealing with the relationship between humanity and nature. This concept is also encapsulated by the Japanese word nagare, meaning "stream," and leads to the realization of vital connections between the divine nature of the kami in the natural world, and humanity through respectful rituals; between post-mortem souls and the living such as the ancestor/descendent linkage; and between the inner and outer worlds. The ancient Japanese did not precisely demarcate their world into the material and the spiritual, nor between this world and another perfect realm. Miyazaki boldly expressed his Shinto based philosophy inherited from Norinaga, saying in an interview about *Princess Mononoke* that "I've come to the point where I just can't make a movie without addressing the problem of humanity as part of an ecosystem."

---

13 Moto-ori Norinaga. Kojiki-den (Commentaries on the Kojiki), 1764.

Miyazaki's Characters & Shinto Archtypes

Moonvoice Ravenari (2006) made a discussion about Miyazaki's characters from psycho-analytical insights. He introduces the theorists like Hanegraaf (1996), O'Connor (1985) and Burnett (1991) as he made his arguments."[14] In neo-paganism, Hanegraaf (1996) believes that 'in Jungian fashion, the 'gods' of traditional pantheons are often interpreted as archetypes and the traditional religious concepts are reinterpreted in psychological terms as psychology itself is "embedded in an encompassing religious framework." The idea that the films of Hayao Miyazaki carry archetypes of paganism within a Shinto setting is supported by the universality of archetypes (O'Connor, 1985). Jung noticed this universality by turning to mythologies in world-wide religions that are considered 'pagan', including the "Elgonian peoples of East Africa and the Pueblo people of North America"(Burnett, 1991). [15]

Archetypes, an old concept that was revived with the theories and practices of Carl Jung, can be understood as:

The necessity, to apprehend and experience life in a manner conditioned by the past history of mankind....archetypal images are the symbolic representation of the archetypes or these primordial patterns or modes of pre-existent apprehension (O'Connor, 1985, p. 23).

The Jungian concept of the archetype can be understood as being the manifestation of an unconscious or subconscious "myth-creating level of the mind" that creates a myth or god-form by which to live in order to reconcile the opposing conscious and subconscious (ibid. p. 89). This helps

---

14 Moonvoice Ravenari. Everything's Too Cold, but You're so Hot. Live Journal thesis on Miyazaki stuff, 2006. Online at http://community.livejournal.com/ghibli/161880.html
15 Moonvoice Ravenari, 2006. Ibid.

understand individuation narratives (ibid.) Individuation is considered a psychological goal to reconcile internal opposites, such as the subconscious and conscious, or our shadow, irrational self with our objective, rational self in order to become whole (ibid. p 14). It allows us to recognize that each person possesses the potential for great growth and destruction.

Archetypes express individuation narratives and help to understand how one might reconcile one's own individuation of the self. There are many classic archetypes such as King, Warrior, Magna Mater, Innocent (ibid.; Barrett, 1989). Archetypes have been accepted whole-heartedly by many modern – and traditional – practitioners of paganism and are often activated through spiritual initiation processes (Burnett, 1991, p. 134). This activation is a realization of the presence of varying archetypes through rituals that may exalt the presence of the Warrior or God within the male and the presence of the Goddess or Mother within the female. Other archetypes can also be acknowledged via ritual and initiation.[16]

Jungian psychologists maintain that since the western world is a community grounded in non-mystical, transcendent Christianity, it tends to disregard the subconscious. In this culture we can become 'distanced from primordial archetypes' (Burnett, 1991, p. 116-117). It is feasible then, that the reintroduction of popular children's animations that feature subversive pagan themes and archetypes would re-connect children and adults alike with ideas of the different archetypes available, and the individuation that these archetypes can bring forth.

Typical archetypes in Miyazaki's anime and manga are *the Shaman/*Shamaness, *the Chaste Heroine*, *the Animist*

---
16 Moonvoice Ravenari, 2006. Ibid.

Warrior, the Greedy Magna Mater, the Benevolent Kami, the Impartial Kami and *the Destructive Kami*. Of these seven the Shamaness is the most common to Shinto tradition (Earhart, 1974, p. 89-97). The Shaman/Shamaness is the 'wise-man/woman'. He or she is typically old, a great-grandfather/grandmother figure with grey hair and somewhat grotesque appearance. The Shaman/Shamaness as archetype can be characterized by the following traits; he or she is the custodian of ancestral knowledge and the customs of the people; he or she has final say in his or her domain and is venerated. The Shaman/Shamaness works via divinatory rites and oracles such as runes and often uses extra-sensory perception or pre-sentience (Hori, 1968, p. 30).[17] He/she can be interpreted in neo-pagan or modern pagan mythologies as a manifestation of the Crone archetype, or the post-menopausal dark goddess latent in everyone, particularly older women (Burnett, 1991). In Miyazaki's narratives, some of typical Shamaness archetypes are Obaba, from *Nausicaä* and Hii-sama, from Princess Mononoke, Yubaaba and Zeniba from Spirited Away, and the nanny in My Neighbour Totoro.[18]

The second of these seven pagan archetypes from Miyazaki's films is the manifestation of the Chaste Heroine. Strong, female heroines were quite rare in Japanese films before, and archetypes within film (Barrett, 1989), however the trend is changing more in contemporary times. Miyazaki has been using strong, female leads in his animated features since the early 1980s when he released *Nausicaä of the Valley of the Wind*. The presence of strong, independent heroines in Miyazaki's work tends to be considered quite distinct in a western society which is considered patriarchal, where it is rare for aggressive, war-like women to be partnered with pacifistic

---

[17] Hori, I.. Folk Religion in Japan: Continuity and Change (Chicago: The University of Chicago Press, (1968).

[18] Moonvoice Ravenari. Everything's Too Cold, but You're so Hot. Live Journal thesis on Miyazaki stuff, 2006. Online at http://community.livejournal.com/ghibli/161880.html

men (Tucker, 2005). The Chaste Heroine is usually isolated from a community or from human company by choice. She also facilitates positive change in herself and/or others, being virginal and often 'wild,' supported by the Animist Warrior, having a significant ability to communicate respectfully with the kami. In neo-paganism she can be considered the manifestation of the Maiden archetype from the three-fold Goddess (Burnett, 1991). She is a pagan archetype easily understood, as she is quite flawed but determined to help her society and herself. Her accessibility is also due to her being universally pagan, instead of specifically Shinto. She is capable of murder, brutality, being temperamental and petty, yet is also compassionate, determined and innocent. The typical chaste heroines in Miyazaki's film and manga are Nausicaä, from *Nausicaä of the Valley of the Wind*; Chihiro, from Spirited Away; and Princess Mononoke/San, from Princess Mononoke.

The third of the seven pagan archetypes is the Animist Warrior. The Animist Warrior isn't specific to Shinto in historic mythology, but is a universally pagan archetype with the ideals of respecting nature, kami worship and animism. He can be considered the neo-pagan manifestation of the Warrior, an archetype also recognized by Jung (Burnett, 1991; O'Connor, 1985). His individuation narrative is very comprehensible and self explanatory. Animist warrior is a pagan archetype that is more universally understandable. Through this archetype Miyazaki has been able to strongly convey Shinto motif of respect for the land and the spiritual world. The Animist Warrior believes that all life is sacred, and will fight or defend the land and the kami. He defends the Chaste Heroine and acts as a catalyst for the Heroine's growth. The Animist Warrior, like the Chaste Heroine, is an ostracized character. Typical manifestations of the Animist Warrior archetype were in the form of Haku, from Spirited Away; and Ashitaka, from Princess Mononoke.

The fourth pagan archetype is the Greedy Magna Mater, a manifestation of the Mother archetype in the three-fold Goddess within neo-paganism (Burnett, 1991). The Magna Mater, or mothering/nurturing aspect of womanhood, is an archetype coined originally by Jung and represents the all-mother of death and rebirth, from which all living being were coming to this world and returning to (O'Connor, 1985, p. 27). In Miyazaki's films the mother is concerned with material desire while still remaining nurturing and kindly to a degree. She is often the 'villain' or antagonist to humanity, though she is not evil and her moral code is somewhat ambivalent. The Greedy Magna Mater is characterized by her need to plunder the land and/or kami for riches and/or power. She protects the people within her establishment fiercely, with a great sense of compassion and propriety. She is an extremely 'human' manifestation of all archetypes, living in a community closely to her people and displaying many human characteristics. She makes mistakes, poor decisions; however, is the archetype most capable of redemption. Since her mentality is mega consumerism, she is relevant on a global scale, but particularly easy to emphasize with in western culture.. The presence of this archetype assisted Miyazaki to communicate the problems of greed in light of Shinto spirituality. The Greedy Magna Mater archetype manifests within Lady Kushana, from Nausicaä; Yubaaba, from Spirited Away; Lady Eboshi, from Princess Mononoke.

The fifth pagan archetype is the Benevolent Kami, a Shinto manifestation of a kami that supports human endeavour and is benevolent to human-kind. Kami are diverse, and harmony is thought to be achieved when they work cooperatively with each other – but not necessarily in harmony with humans, which is why there are also manifestations of indifferent or even antagonistic kami (Ono, 1962, p. 7-9). The Benevolent Kami 'rejoice in the evidence of harmony and cooperation in this world' (ibid. p. 7). They are characterized in Miyazaki's films as being kind or friendly to humans and facilitating the growth, contentment, joy and peace within human community. Benevolent Kami are less accessible as archetypes as they feature no individuation story or reconciling of opposites and are almost an exclusive Shinto manifestation. They become more accessible to western audiences in the way they facilitate the individuation narratives of other archetypes. The Benevolent Kami can be seen in the Kodamas (tree spirits) in *Princess Mononoke*; and Haku, from *Spirited Away*. Other examples of the Benevolent Kami can be seen in Totoro, immortal and gigantic cat-like creatures from *My Neighbour Totoro*.

The Impartial Kami is the sixth archetype to be discussed. As a kami, this Shinto archetype is a guardian spirit of the land, or aspects of the land. The loyalty of the Impartial Kami to the land compromises their need or wants to help humans, and can lead to wanton destruction of humans. The Impartial Kami has the following characteristics; it displays little affection towards humans, is concerned with life/death cycles and it is the catalyst for change in the Chaste Heroine, Animist Warrior and the community. This particular archetype is the least accessible and potentially destructive. It is destructive because it values land above the integrity of humans. In western culture this evaluation is unusual because in Christian conditioning the creator gives mankind the dominant status over the land and rest of creation through the Dominion Covenant (Genesis 1:28). The Impartial Kami manifests in the following characters in Miyazaki's films like Moro the wolf god, from *Princess Mononoke*, and the Ohmu, from *Nausicaä of the Valley of the Wind* and Shishigami in *Princess Mononoke*.

Finally, the seventh archetype to be discussed is destructive and demonic Kami. It is an archetype not from the traditional Shinto from antiquity, but a product of modern State Shinto, which incorporated Western philosophies of the Enlightenment into traditional Shinto belief after Meiji Restoration, which took place in 1868. Japan's State Shinto became the foundation of Japan's nationalism and forced all Japanese citizens to worship the emperor, as a Kami in person. The State Shinto professed that the emperor was a divine despot in the same sense as the Roman Caesar was proclaimed prior to the Christian era. These demonic Kami are products of engineering by the leadership of Meiji government and led the entire nation of Japan into self-destruction by 1945. The destructive Kami can be seen in God-Warrior from Nausicaä and Daitarabocchi or Shishigami after losing his head.

Nausicaä Synopsis

Nausicaä of the Valley of the Wind (風の谷のナウシカ) Kaze no tani no Naushika) was released by Japanese manga writer and filmmaker Hayao Miyazaki, based on his manga of the same name. The movie carries underlying environmentalist messages and was presented by the World Wide Fund for Nature when it came to the market in 1984.

The story takes place 1,000 years after a global war known as the "Seven Days of Fire", an event which destroyed the entire human civilization and most of the Earth's ecosystem. Only a small remnant of humanity survived, forming a few settlements scattered around, isolated from one another by the Sea of Decay (腐海 fukai). Literally translating as the Rotting Sea or the Sea of Fungus, the Sea of Decay is a lethally toxic jungle of fungus swarming with gigantic insects named Ohmu, which seem to come together only to wage war.

The primary protagonist, Nausicaä, the only surviving child of King Jil, ruler of the Valley of the Wind, is a charismatic young princess of the peaceful community by the Sea of Decay. Her name comes from the princess Nausicaä in the Odyssey who assisted Odysseus, and is transcribed into Japanese as ナウシカ. Part of her character comes from a Japanese folk hero and a character in a collection of short stories, 堤中納言物語 the "Tsutsumi-chunagon Monogatari" compiled in the 13th century, known as "the princess who loved insects" (虫めづる姫君 Mushimezuru Himegimi), while another part was inspired by the writings of Bernard Evslin (1922-1993) the Greek Mythology specialist, as he had written a more in-depth extrapolation of Odyssey's Nausicaä.

Although a skillful warrior princess like Xena whom Hollywood created in the1990s, Miyazaki's Nausicaä is humane and fundamentally peace-loving. She has an unusual gift for communicating with all creatures, particularly with the Ohmu, the gigantic, armored, caterpillar-like insects who are the most intelligent creatures in the Sea of Decay and the Impartial Kami archetype of this story.

She is also noted for her empathy toward all living beings including humans, animals and other creatures. She is an intelligent girl with scholarly curiosity, and inspired by the mentor figure named Yupa, a wandering samurai type warrior possessed of great wisdom. Nausicaä frequently explores the Sea of Decay and conducts scientific experiments in an attempt to understand the true nature and origins of the toxic world in which she lives. Her explorations of the nature are facilitated by her skill at "windriding"; flying with an advanced glider-like craft with a jet assist called a möwe.

The Valley of the Wind is threatened when another state, Pejite, unearths a God Warrior embryo which is then stolen by a more powerful state, Tolmekia. The God Warriors are one of the lethal, giant, bio-mechanical weapons used in the ancient war. Both Pejite and Tolmekia hope to use the God Warrior against each other and, ultimately, against the Sea of Decay. While transporting the embryo back to their realm, the Tolmekian troops led by Lady Kushana the Greedy Magna Mater archetype of this story are attacked by insects and subsequently crash-land in the Valley. The very next day, the Tolmekians invade the Valley to secure and revive the Warrior, eventually forcing the peaceful people of the Valley into armed resistance. The situation deteriorates as the fight to possess the God Warrior escalates out of control and the Sea of Decay strikes back against those who attack it.

The story holds deeper meaning than a simple depiction of war and violence. The film contains the indepth description of humanity, ecological subtexts in Miyazaki's narrative and the theme of Shinto archetypes. Miyazaki describes even the insects as kami who are working toward some secret harmony and even the lethal fungal forest seems to have a vital role in Earth's new ecosystem.

Shinto Motif in Nausicaä

Nausicaä's world, despite being a post-apocalyptic world in the 30th century, somehow resembles Medieval Europe, and is saturated with Shinto tradition and imagery. It features a blind Shamaness who has an ability to prophesy, a trait common to Shinto Shamanesses. Throughout the whole story of Nausicaä, there is a theme that morality according to Shinto is linked with cleanliness and freedom from pollution.

In order to illustrate the moral world of the ancient Japanese, the creation myth of Izanagi and Izanami in the Kojiki plays out notions of good and evil, purity and pollution. The myth goes like this: when Izanami gave birth to the kami of fire, she suffered greatly and eventually "died" and entered "yomi-no-kuni," the realm of the dead. Izanagi missed her so greatly that he followed her into the netherworld to take her back to the world of living. As they traveled back to the world where they came from, she warned Izanagi not to look upon her in such a state of pollution or death that lasts until she gets out of the underworld. But he was so in love with her and looked upon her prior to crossing the River of Yomi which separated the realm of the living and dead. When she discovered that he had broken his promise, she turned into an evil and vengefully goddess and pursued him and he barely escaped. This story that Izanagi's lovely wife turned into an evil deity simply because she was polluted as she went down to Hades illustrates eloquently the Shinto concept of polution and evil.

In his studies of this ancient text, Norinaga (1764) used this story to draw several conclusions about the moral world of the ancient Japanese.[19] He contends that the Japanese word "tsumi," that means "evil," encompasses more than just moral transgressions. It also implies spiritual and physical impurity or filthiness, including natural disasters, disease and death. Secondly, such evils should be ritually purified or cleansed. And finally, good encompasses spiritual and physical cleanliness and harmony with the surrounding environment. In the ancient Kojiki, the words for good - akashi (bright), kiyoshi (pure, clean) and naoshi (upright) were used interchangeably.

Hence, the true purpose of purification according to Norinaga is to remove what is evil or polluted, in order that something good or bright can take its place. Such a moral universe with no concept of original sin that was implanted into human DNA by the enemyis quite different from Shinto. Shinto holds that the nature of humanity is considered essentially good and pure and the evil does not stain one's soul. Therefore, Shinto views that evil will be removed simply by the purification rite and does not see the necessity of a Messiah or redeemer who surgically removes the evil out of humanity in a more drastic way.

---

19 Moto-ori Norinaga. Kojiki-den (Commentaries on the Kojiki), 1764.

Miyazaki has said that the pollution of Minamata Bay with mercury in the 1950s and 1960s was one major event that inspired him to write Nausicaä. Because of serious health concerns, people stopped fishing in the bay, but strangely the fish stocks in the area increased dramatically. Miyazaki said the news "sent shivers up my spine," and he was greatly impressed by the resilience of other living creatures. Fish around Minamata Bay could absorb such poison and survived just like Ohmu and other creatures in the Sea of Decay.

In the 30th century world of Nausicaä, the world had been utterly destroyed in The Seven Days of Fire by a great holocaust inflicting all humans. Yet, the land is abundant with life, although badly damaged by massive radioactive substance. Toxins have caused all plants and insects on earth to mutate into more resilient and formidable species. Ohmu a giant breed of intelligent insects arise to rule the planet, and a new ecosystem, poisonous to humans, is established. Humans hate the new ecosystem, calling it the Sea of Corruption, the Toxic Jungle, the Acid Sea and the Wasteland since it is uninhabitable for them. This kind of ecological influence is apparent in Nausicaä's many symbolic moments that, as Paul Wells (b. 1966) a Canadian journalist and columnist suggests, "become the locus for narrational emphasis and the nexus of spiritual and philosophic ideas." As well as carrying a prophetic trope, the character of the princess embodies certain ideas about how to live with the natural world. Her characterization can be read as signifying transitional and purifying aspects as a Shinto priestess with unusual power rather than any messianic figure that Westerners may conceive, except she sacrificed her life to save the world.

In the very first part of Nausicaä film, the heroine circles high above a verdant landscape in her white glider. She descends lightly and enters the other worldly forest, walking through strange looking caves, collecting phosphorescent plant samples, and discovering the shed carapace of one of the giant intelligent insects, Ohmu. In this whimsical exploration of her world with child-like curiosity, Nausicaä takes a scientific and beatific interest in the forest. This attitude parallels the Shinto world-view expressed by Norinaga (1764): "this heaven and earth and all things therein are without exception strange and marvelous when examined carefully."[20] He sees the wonders of all things in this universe as "kami-given," and in the world of Nausicaä, the princess' distinct and heroic attributes are characterized by her ability to see this essentially good nature in all things. While other characters either fiercely attack the forest or avoid it completely, Nausicaä lives with it in harmony, since she is able to see what Norinaga called magokoro, "the sincere heart," in all creatures there.

Nausicaä views that pollution does not come from the reversal of power relations between humans and insects, but rather through the interruption of the continuity or "nagare" – the flow of nature. The violent Tolmekians and Pejites, with their insistence on using drastic weapons from antiquity, continue to fight against the forest and each other. Commander Kushana of Tolmekian goes to the extreme of rousing a dormant God Warrior that has lain under the earth for millennia. And the Pejites torture an Ohmu infant in order to provoke the adult Ohmu on a murderous rampage through the Valley to attack Tolmekians. The people of the Valley are terrified by what has been done. Obaba, a blind shamaness who acts like Nausicaä's grandmother says; "The anger of the Ohmu is the anger of the earth. Of what use is surviving, relying on a thing like the God Warrior?"

The Ohmu and the princess also share an important link in terms of purification. In her personal laboratory, Nausicaä has been growing spores obtained from the forest. Given clean water and soil, she finds that the fungi and plants do

---
20 Moto-ori Norinaga, 1764. ibid.

not produce poisonous vapours. She comes to the conclusion that it is the soil that is toxic, not the plants that grow in it. Later, after an aerial battle, she crash-lands in the forest and discovers that there is in a subterranean cavern of clean water and non-toxic sands. She and a Pejite boy whom she is trying to save realize that the entire forest operates as a purifying organism; the trees absorb the poisons from the soil, crystalize and neutralize them, before eventually dissolving into sand. The Toxic Forest that people hate badly is effectively purifying the planet.

The Ohmu are aware of this and act to defend the forest, and thus the earth, from humans. The Ohmu that represent the archetype of Impartial Kami are intricately connected to the new ecosystem and able to feel telepathically the pain of all other creatures in the forest, not just their own kind. Despite suffering from the aggression of the Tolmekians and Pejites, the Ohmu do not attempt a vengeance. They acknowledge the sacrifice Nausicaä makes by returning life to her body and see her "magokoro."

Shinto Archetypes & Nausicaä

Obaba, a blind elderly woman from Nausicaä of the Valley of the Wind, is a Shamaness according to Earhart's (1974) definition. She is the "Kuchiyose" or a shamaness who engages in divinatory rites, often settles in villages and is usually blind.[21]

Obaba is a custodian of the custom and tradition of the lore, and admonishes Nausicaä for not knowing the prophecy of the 'saviour' of all the lands. She plays an important role by demonstrating her knowledge of lore. This is reflected both at the beginning and end of the movie, where she acts as prophetess on behalf of the people. She has final say over

---

21 H. B. Earhart. The Religious Life of Man: Religion in the Japanese Experience; Sources and Interpretations,1974. Ibid.

the operations of the village. She is the one who declares the forest is dead and must be burnt. As the custodian of the prophecy that will save the people, Obaba uses extra-sensory perception to divine the air around her and perform divinatory rites. She has a close relationship to the spirits of the land and its sacredness when she says; 'the earth knows it's wrong for us to survive if we have to depend on a monster like that,' when the Tolmekians threaten the land with a man-made monster.

Nausicaä is the protagonist within Nausicaä, and an excellent manifestation of the Chaste Heroine. She is partially isolated from the community and human company by choice, although she is a respected princess who lives among people in the Valley of the Wind. Nausicaä has her own privacy in which she is isolated from all human contact as she walks through the toxic jungle, while at the same time living among her people. She is virginal and shown as having no romantic attachments to boys, nor any pressure to have romantic relationships. She is also wild and feels at home in the toxic forest. She often risks her life to save her people, such as standing on a flying aircraft twice to present herself as a moving target to gunfire, and fiercely defending Lord Jihl, her father. When he dies, Nausicaä is so infuriated that she slaughters several armoured soldiers with a cane. She has an exceptional gift to communicate with creatures of the forest and the Ohmu. Lord Yupa, the great swordsman, comments on this ability, 'what a mysterious power she has.' She respects the Ohmu and often communicates with them often telepathically. She facilitates positive change in herself and her community and eventually saves the entire earth from destruction by sacrificing her life.

Lady Kushana is the Greedy Magna Mater and a protective mother-figure who wishes to save the earth through destructive means of her own. However, she plunders the land, and squanders the Wind Valley's resources, so that the villagers are infuriated. She destroys Ohmu, cities, and digs deep into the earth to excavate a dormant god-warrior for her own sinister purposes. She protects her people, and desires to unite the remaining kingdoms - 'our goal is to unify the kingdom's surrounding Tolmekia, and build a world of prosperity.' She makes bad choices but is ultimately not without redemption. She is portrayed as having villainous qualities, but is a very human character with positive character traits at the same time.

The Ohmu, the giant insects from Nausicaä, are Impartial Kami. They are the guardian spirits of the toxic forest that is hated by humans, and they defend it with their lives. They display little affection towards humans and are feared throughout the earth for devastating entire cities and indiscriminately killing when rageful. Obaba says of their rage; "People tried time and again to burn the toxic forest, but time and again their attempts did nothing but enrage the Ohmu...they could not be stopped."

At the same time their rage protects the plants in the forest that sucks all the poisons out of the air that is killing humans. In a roundabout way, the Ohmu are guardians of humans. They facilitate some of the greatest change in acting to completely purify and restore the earth. At the end of the story, they save the life of Nausicaä, who becomes the embodiment of the peace forged between insects and humans.

Spirited Away Synopsis

Spirited Away is the story of a young Japanese girl named Chihiro, who, with her parents, is moving to a new city. They pass an old "Torii" or a traditional Japanese gate commonly found at the entry to a Shinto shrine, leaning against a large tree, surrounded by numerous "spirit houses." The road leads to a tunnel-like entrance of an abandoned theme park. They end up at a restaurant full of delicious food, but no people are present. Chihiro's parents start eating food, but she is reluctant to eat without permission of the restaurant owner. Outside she meets a young boy named Haku, who tells her to leave the place as soon as possible. Puzzled, she runs to get her parents, but they are still eating and to her horror, have turned into pigs. Unable to leave -- the river bed is now filled with water -- she is comforted and helped by Haku, who escorts her through a strange realm of "ghosts and goblins," a world of wondrous creatures who have come to bathe and be refreshed in the bathhouse run by an old woman named Yubāba 湯婆婆 (yu 湯 is "hot water," baba 婆婆 is "old woman"). Eventually Yubāba steals Chihiro's 千尋 name (*chi* 千 is 1000, *hiro* 尋 is "inquire, fathom, look for," so Chihiro can mean "looking deeply," or "inquiring after many things") in the realm of oblivion. Yubāba gives her a new name – Sen 千 (an alternate reading of the same written character), which she is commanded to use.[22]

Sen encounters many other strange creatures, including Kamaji, an old man with six arachnid limbs who looks like Spiderman's grandfather with three bouncing body-less heads, a Oshira-sama or daikon sumo-sized god creature with fingers like daikon radishes, and a group of Kasuga-sama apparitions dressed in classic court attire with white square masks. There also several non-human creatures such as "frog men" and "slug women," a ryūjin or a huge white dragon; and a most mysterious black, shadowy, ambivalent figure named Kaonashi or "No Face." Many of these creatures come from Japanese folklores and mythology. For instance, daikon radish farmers worship Oshirasama and pray for abundant harvest in the fall.

The experiences in the strange world make Sen's character stronger. She increasingly becomes courageous and stands

[22] James W. Boyd and Tetsuya Nishimura. Shinto Perspectives in Miyazaki's Anime Film "Spirited Away." The Journal of Religion and Film, 2004.

her ground firmly but politely in a number of frightening and dangerous encounters. She eventually helps Haku, whose alternate form is a white dragon, to remember his original name and true identity. Sen, not forgetting her real name is Chihiro because she has written it on her belongings, is eventually able to leave the place after passing a final test by Yubāba. When they return to the bath house along with Bo, Haku demands that Yubaba fulfill her side of the deal, she cannot break the spell unless rules are followed. Sen is told to identify her parents among a group of pigs, but sees that none of them are her parents and is soon reunited with her real human parents. At the end of the story, her father asks if she is up to the challenges of a new home and new school. A more self-confident Chihiro responds "I think I can handle it."[23] In this film, there is a strong overtone of the Jungian theme of individuation narrative to reconcile our opposing conscious and subconscious. Psychologists might view the strange world she has experienced as representing the subconscious realm of her mind and Sen as her alter ego. While Chihiro resided in the same strange mythological world as Sen and grappled through various events to manage the tasks given to her, she went through the process of self individuation and psychological growth and developed the new ego-strength at the end of the movie. All non-human creatures and spiritual beings she encountered facilitated her learning experiences and personal growth.

Also, it is significant that the strange incident happens to Chihiro in her transitional time when she is moving to a new city and starting a new life. People often have to go through the self individuation process and deal with various psychological problems in both conscious and subconscious realm when they move to a new stage of life.

---

[23] Her last statement, "I think I can handle it" is found only in English dubbed version. However, the viewers could observe her newly acquired confidence also in the original Japanese version, although she didn't made such statement.

Shinto Motif in Spirited Away

There are many folk and Shrine Shinto perspectives embedded in the cultural vocabulary of this film. The director Miyazaki explicitly acknowledges his indebtedness to this tradition. He refers, for example, to his "very warm appreciation for the various, very humble rural Shinto rituals that continue to this day throughout rural Japan" and cites the solstice rituals when villagers call forth all the local kami and invite them to bathe in their baths twice in a year. This, apparently, is the inspiration for Yubaba's bathhouse locale in the film, and his reference to kami invokes the essence of the Shinto tradition.

The first indication that Chihiro is about to enter a realm of the extra-ordinary is her wide-eyed glimpse of the torii, leaning against an old tree, surrounded by little house-like shrines. In Shinto tradition, a torii is a symbol of superior potency that can initiate changes in one's life. But to benefit from the kami presence that inhabits such a place, one must be sensitized to their presence. This can occur if one experientially moves from the mundane and everyday world into a liminal realm. As Van Gennep (1873 - 1957) and Turner (1920 – 1983) have explained, in order to become something new, one first has to abandon the old, move through a liminal phase that is neither here nor there, and then return -- but as one who is "re-formed" into a new persona. In the Japanese context it takes a cleansing -- a wiping away of the external and interior pollution that inhibits us, to arrive at such a fresh and dynamic condition.[24]

Like Alice in Wonderland who falls through a rabbit hole into a strange realm, or Dorothy in the Wizard of Oz who follows the yellow brick road, Chihiro together with her parents walks

---

24 Arnold van Gennep. The Rites of Passage. (Chicago: University of Chicago Press, 1909/1960); Victor W. Turner. The Ritual Process: Structure and Anti-Structure. (Chicago: Aldine, 1969).

through a tunnel-like passage and across a dry river bed into a realm characterized by disorientation, ambiguity and a sense of otherness. For an engaged audience, the film itself, through its own artistry, can affect a sense of disorientation and liminal space or a threshold of a different dimension of the universe.

The Japanese title of the film explicitly indicates this threshold to a different realm of existence. The last phrase in the title 千と千尋の神隠し "Sen to Chihiro no kami-kakushi" literally means "Sen and Chihiro hidden by kami." There is the expression in Japanese 神隠しに遭う "kami-kakushi ni au" (to experience kami-kakushi) that refers to someone being inexplicably missing for some time. If and when that person returns and whether or not that person remembers what has happened while being gone – people refer to that person as "hidden by the kami." Chihiro's parents do not remember being gone and transformed into swine. Their car is covered with leaves and dust when they find it because a considerable length of time has passed. But they have no idea how much time they spent in a strange world. But Chihiro herself does remember her transforming journey into a realm of the kami. Miyazaki refers to this idea: "In my grandparents' time it was believed that spirits or Kami existed everywhere -- in trees, rivers, insects, wells, anything. My generation does not believe this, but I like the idea that we should all treasure everything because spirits might exist there, and we should treasure everything because there is a kind of life to everything."

Among the various ghost-like creatures in the film are the wandering souls of dead persons who appear in this world due to past regrets or obsessions. But a more haunting figure in the film is the Kaonashi or "No Face". He likely represents the type of person who has little interest in things, is gloomy and melancholic, and subject to morbid introspection. No Face is lonely and unsuccessfully seeks Chihiro's friendship by offering her the semblance of shining gold nuggets. Her polite refusal to accept, however, turns No Face into a horrendous monster.

But No Face is not a fixed figure of evil. Toward the end of the film he begins to learn from Yubāba's twin sister Zenība how to improve his attitude and act with "makoto," genuine "sincerity," toward others as he makes an effort to protect Chihiro. Kaonashi could represent a ghost of a person who has not received genuine love, compassion and care from others and has died in misery.

At the climax of the film, Chihiro remembers when as a toddler she lost a pink shoe in a river and almost drowned trying to retrieve it, but was carried by the water's current to the safety of the shore. She realizes the river was the Kohaku River, and that this is Haku's true name --an identity which he could not remember because the river had been filled in and covered with buildings[25]. When she explains this to Haku -- now in the form of a white river dragon -- he remembers his name.

As Victor Turner notes, there can be moments in the liminal experience of deep reciprocal encounters between persons or places, i.e. a deep sense of mutual relation (I -Thou) between persons or with nature. Miyazaki is possibly portraying Chihiro as being in a genuine, authentic relation with the kami presence of the Kohaku River.[26]

The character of Haku is in some respects the embodiment of so called traditional Japanese cultural values. His attire resembles that of the noble men in Heian period (794 - 1185). He wears something similar to a hakama, part of a Shinto priest's formal costume. Besides this courtly dress, his speech

---

[25] It is likely Miyazaki's environmentalist message and critique of the over-building in Japan at the expense of nature.
[26] Victor W. Turner.The Ritual Process: Structure and Anti-Structure (Chicago: Aldin, 1969).

is formal and somehow old fashioned.[27] When he refers to himself, he does not use the more colloquial "boku" but the more formal "watashi." And when he addresses Sen, he uses the ancient, nobler aristocratic term "sonata." In fact, Haku's full name, "Nigihayami kohaku-nushi," is reminiscent of a reference in the Kojiki, the oldest extant book in Japanese, to "Nigi-haya-mi-no-mikoto" the name of an ancestor to one of the families of high courtly rank in ancient times.

In Shinto, there is no clear demarcation between the Kami and spirits of the dead, and many Kami used to be humans when they were alive. If Haku was Kami evolved from the dead, he must be a person in Heian period or historical "Nigi-haya-mi-no-mikoto" who lived in the Yamato era (300AD - 710 AD).

Haku, who embodies certain traditional values, helps Chihiro in the transitional world, and that Chihiro in turn helps Haku to remember his identity. Perhaps Miyazaki is affirming to contemporary viewers of this anime film some important insights into the Shinto Japanese tradition represented by Haku, that can be helpful in these modern times.

Shinto Archtypes & Spirited Away

As all characters in the film are all kami, or guardian spirits and non-human creatures – with the exception of Chihiro and her parents – it is feasible that this particular narrative is rich in Shinto/pagan archetypes. Spirited Away features both Yubaaba and Zeniba as Shamaness archetypes, and Yubaaba is also the Greedy Magna Mater. She is for this reason both a complex set of archetypes and an equally complex character. Chihiro is the Chaste Heroine, and Haku is the Animist Warrior and Benevolent Kami at the same time.[28]

---

27 In Englished dubbed version, his speech was translated into modern English. I wonder his old fashioned overtone could be better preserved if his speech is dubbed into older English like Shakespeare.

28 Moonvoice Ravenari, 2006. Ibid.

Unlike Nausicaä and San from *Princess Mononoke*, Chihiro from *Spirited Away* is a weaker example of the Chaste Heroine archetype, as she is not as wild as the other Chaste Heroines, nor is she introduced as having an innate connection with the kami. Later in the movie, however, she forms a tight friendship with Haku, a water dragon and river kami. She forms a respectful relationship with another river dragon called Stink Spirit and her compassion when bathing him leads to her being rewarded. She is isolated from her parents and close friends throughout the movie. She could be considered the Child-Maiden who is still in a process of growing into the Chaste Heroine. Chihiro facilitates positive change within herself while she is in the strange world. She becomes more mature and independent when she learns how to clean the bathtubs. She becomes compassionate when she becomes friends with Haku and addresses the Stink Spirit. She saves the bath-house from ruin when she stops No-Face devouring everything there, recovers him from his monstrous evolution, and takes him to Zeniba's house. She also saves the life of Haku and frees him from Yubaaba's spell when she returns his name to him and facilitates his own evolution into independence. The main focus of this film appears to be the theme of individuation narratives coming from Chihiro's mysterious experience as Sen. This gives the audience a clue how they might reconcile their own individuation of self according to the O'Connor (1985) study.

As an Animist Warrior, Haku defends the Chaste Heroine fervently. He tries to save her from the bath-house and helps her survive there. He saves her from Yubaaba, and gives her the courage to realize that she can make it. He gives her back her clothes with her name on it and real human food that nourishes her. He makes the deal with Yubaaba to ensure Chihiro's safe return to her parents if the beloved baby Boo returns safely from Zeniba's place. He has no family, and is unable to return home – like Ashitaka in *Princess Mononoke*

– his river where he was guardian was filled in by mankind. Haku is also a Benevolent Kami, a white river dragon, or river kami. He is able to shape-shift between the form of human and dragon, and possesses power over the land, water and wind. He is Chihiro's friend and confidante who keeps on telling her not to give up. Many of his positive kami aspects can be seen in his support of her as demonstrated in his role as Animist Warrior. He is very benevolent and nurturing towards Chihiro, and facilitates her growth.

To Chihiro, Haku is also a unique guardian who happens to be a Prince Charming and Dirty Old Man at the same time, in the same way as Angel to Buffy in *Buffy the Vampire Slayer* (1997)[29] a popular American TV series.[30] Haku looks only a few years older than her, but in fact, nearly two thousand years older. When Chihiro loses a pink shoe as an infant in the Kohaku River and almost drowns trying to retrieve it, Haku was already adult Kami much older than any living human. If he were ever a human in the past like "Nigi-haya-mi-no-mikoto" who lived in Yamato era (300AD - 710 AD), he was born over 1,700 years ago. Haku, who retains youth forever, may be the realization of Miyazaki's own ego ideal, which is an Animist Warrior and immortal Kami simultaneously, and serves as a guardian of a young girl.

Yubaaba is a Shamaness like her sister Zeniba, but also a Greedy Magna Mater. She is a character of contradictions; she is deeply concerned with making money and jewels from her kami clients, and surrounds herself in her private office with jewels, gold coins and other aspects of wealth which she continues to accumulate. She is villainous; she turns Chihiro's parents into pigs and threatens to 'eat them for bacon.' She

---

29 James South, B. Pasley, Jeffrey L. et al. Buffy the Vampire Slayer and Philosophy (London, UK: Open Court Publishing Company, 2003).

30 Angel is a good Vampire who has a human soul and helped Buffy to fight evil monster as her guardian. He is over 200 years older than her although maintaining a youthful appearance. Angel once told Buffy's mother, "I am old enough to be her ancestor."

threatens to turn Chihiro into soot, and deliberately places her in dangerous situations. But at the same time, she displays maternal love for her baby Boo, whom she cares for above anything else. While she is villainized, the fact that she is the identical twin to the benevolent Zeniba, suggests that Yubaaba herself isn't evil, merely flawed. The Greedy Magna Mater represents the mother archetype inherent in each of us (regardless of gender) that desires to be compassionate, but also to prosper in order to continue such care. This is a highly accessible archetype very appropriate to western consumerist culture. Zenība as a Shamaness heals the soul of Kaonashi, possibly a dead one who has failed to receive genuine love, compassion and care from others in his life time.

The last significant character in this film is Kamaji, an old man with many arms who belongs to the male Shaman archetype. Although he pretends indifference when Sen first meets him, Kamaji helps her to find her way and solve problems throughout the story. Kamaji, who is probably the only male Shaman archetype among all Miyazaki stories, also represents modern men with multiple tasks and no time to rest. He may be the self caricature or the periodic expression of Miyazaki himself who always works and continues to produce manga and films with multiple arachnid limbs, without resting. Perhaps, Miyazaki helps or mentors young women like the Heroine of this film in the same way as Kamaji does.

My Neighbor Totoro Synopsis

My Neighbor Totoro (となりのトトロ Tonari no Totoro) is a 1988 film written and directed by Hayao Miyazaki and produced by Studio Ghibli. The movie won the Animage Anime Grand Prix prize in 1988. An ani-manga version of My Neighbor Totoro was published in English by Viz Communications on November 10, 2004. The film was re-released by Disney on March 7, 2006 featured by a new dub cast. This DVD release is the first version of the film in the United States to include both Japanese and English language tracks, (as Fox did not have the rights to the Japanese audio track for their version.)

The story opens with professor Kusakabe of the University of Tokyo driving a truck with his daughters, Satsuki, 11, and May, 4, down a country road in rural 1950's Tokyo. The family is moving into an old country house near Tokorozawa city in rural Japan in order to be closer to the hospital where his wife is recovering from an illness. It might also provide her a healthier environment. The daughters find the house inhabited by tiny animated dust creatures called "soot sprites," which their father rationalizes as "makkurokurosuke" — an optical illusion seen when moving from light to dark places.[31] These soot spirits are representations of Satsuki and May's apprehensions of moving into a new house. When they become comfortable and are finally able to laugh with their father, the soot spirits leave the house. They start enjoying life there, running around the house exploring, excited at all the room available.

When May, the younger daughter, plays outside the house while her father works inside after Satsuki has left for school, she sees a small translucent white creature with two rabbit-like ears in the grass.[32] Upon following this under the house, she eventually discovers two small magical creatures, which lead her through a briar patch, and into the hollow of a large Camphor Laurel tree.[33] She gives chase to the both of them,

---

31 These creatures are referred to as "dust bunnies" and "soot spirits" in the 1993 English dub; in the Disney version, they are variously called "soot gremlins" or "soot sprites". In the English subtitles of the first Japanese-language version to find its way to America, they were "Black Soots". The original name, "makkurokurosuke", literally means "pitch-black blackie".

32 It gives reminiscent of The White Rabbit from Alice's Adventures in Wonderland to the viewers.

33 Once again it is alluding to Lewis Carrol's rabbit hole.

and they scurry off into a tunnel under the camphor tree. There, she meets and befriends a larger version of the same kind of creature, which identifies itself by a series of roars she interprets as "Totoro." Her father later tells her that this is the "keeper of the forest."

One rainy night, while the girls are waiting for their father's return by bus, Satsuki encounters Totoro for the first time. The girls are worried because their father has not come on the bus they expected, and it is getting late. May insists that she stay with Satsuki until their father returns instead of going back to the house or staying with 'Granny," an old woman neighbour, and she soon falls asleep on Satsuki's back. While they wait, Totoro appears beside them wearing a large leaf on his head and looking rather forlorn. Satsuki offers him the umbrella she had brought along for her father because he has only a leaf on his head. He is delighted and enchanted by the sound of the rain striking the umbrella. When the Catbus, feline-shaped living bus for Totoro, arrives, he hands the girls a package of nuts and seeds and boards his bus.[34]

The girls plant the seeds, that do not sprout for a few days and makes them restless. One night, however, the girls awaken at midnight to find Totoro and his two miniature colleagues engaged in a ritual dance around the planted nuts and seeds. The girls join in, whereupon the seedlings start to sprout and grow at an amazing rate into enormous acorn trees. Totoro then takes his colleagues and the girls for a ride on a magical flying top. In the morning, the girls find that there are no massive trees in their yard, but that the seeds have indeed sprouted.

The final appearance of Totoro in the film occurs when May, believing her mother's condition has worsened, sets off on

---

34 The "nekobasu" or "Catbus" may be referres as a "bio-bus," in the same way as Lexx from *The Lexx* (1997) and some starships from StarTrek are "bio-ships," because they are sentient living organism as well as vehicles.

foot to the hospital and gets lost. Desperate to find her sister, Satsuki returns to the camphor laurel tree and beseeches Totoro to assist her. Delighted to be of assistance, he summons the Catbus, which bounds across the countryside jumping into the tops of trees, rescues May and whisks her and Satsuki over the countryside to see their mother in the hospital. Satsuki realizes that no one else can see the Catbus. At the hospital, Kusakabe explains to her husband that she simply has a light cold and that the hospital might have needlessly worried the children. The girls sit on a tree outside of a hospital, listening to the conversation and discover that their mother is doing well. They deliver an ear of corn, that May believes will make her mother better, and return home on the Catbus. When the Catbus departs, it fades away from the girls' sight in a manner reminiscent of Lewis Carroll's Cheshire Cat.

The closing credits show May and Satsuki's mother returning home and feature scenes of Satsuki and May playing with other children, with Totoro and his friends as unseen bystanders. Miyazaki has asserted that the girls would never see Totoro again, but that the spirits would always be watching over them.

Totoro and Shinto

The film, My Neighbor Totoro (となりのトトロ Tonari no Totoro), has Shintoist themes as most of his other works. In the film, May refers to Totoro as an "obake" or a goblin in Japanese folklores. May says "totoro" and Satsuki asks whether she means a troll. May responds in the affirmative and repeats "totoro", which seems to imply that "totoro" is a childish mispronunciation of the phonetic Japanese pronunciation of "troll" (torōru) ogres in Western myth. This would explain that the film represents Miyazaki's mythological world which mixes traditional Japanese with modern/western influenced elements. While Miyazaki employssome Western component like Totoro's name and Catbus that resembles Cheshire Cat, the core of his philosophical assumption throughout the entire narrative is Shinto based animism as in his other works.

Analyzing characters in light of the archetype theory, "Granny," Kusakabes' neighbor in the Tokorozawa region, is a Shamaness archetype in this film who teaches young Satsuki and May about the spiritual world. Satsuki and May spent their childhood in the early '60s when lifestyles were rapidly changing in Japan and the belief in the spiritual world was beginning to fade. Granny helped the young sisters to rediscover the spiritual beings in the forest and encounter King Totoro, a local Kami who lived in the area over 1,000 years.

Both Satsuki and May are Chaste Heroine archetypes in this film and experience mysterious encounters with Totoro and his family. As heroines, however, they are even weaker than Chihiro. To the young sisters, Totoro is a Benevolent Kami who gave the package of nuts and seeds and take them onboard the Catbus when they need to see their mother. Yet, to others he is an Impartial Kami, a guardian spirit of the land. He displays little affection towards humans except the Kusakabe sisters. He teaches life/death cycles, and confers the purpose of the forest spirit to other kami and facilitates growth of the sisters.[35]

Princess Mononoke Synopsis

Princess Mononoke (もののけ姫 Mononoke Hime) is a Japanese animated film by Hayao Miyazaki, produced through his company, Studio Ghibli, that was first released in Japan in July 1997 and in the United States in October of 1999. Mononoke became the highest grossing movie in

---
35 Moonvoice Ravenari, 2006. Ibid.

Japan until Titanic took over the spot several months later. Overall, Mononoke is the third most popular anime movie in Japan, next to 2001's Spirited Away and 2004's Howl's Moving Castle. Both were also produced by Miyazaki. Roger Ebert placed the movie sixth on his top ten movies of 1999.

It is a jidaigeki (historical drama) set in the late Muromachi period (1336–1573) of Japan, and centers on the struggle between the supernatural guardians of a forest and the humans who consume and often squander its resources, as seen by the outsider Ashitaka. "Mononoke" (物の怪) is not a name, but a general term in Japanese for a spirit or monster.[36]

The storyline of *Princess Mononoke* follows the journey of the last Emishi prince, Ashitaka, and his attempts to make peace between the human settlement, industry, and the creatures living in the surrounding forest.

The film begins with Ashitaka saving his village from an assault by killing the demon form of the boar god Nago. During the fight, Ashitaka receives a demon mark on his right arm and is cursed by the Boar God's hatred and pain. Hii-Sama, the village's old Shamaness, tells Ashitaka that the mark will spread throughout his body, eventually killing him. She tells him that a ball of iron is found inside Nago's corpse that is somehow connected to the curse and suggests that if Ashitaka goes to the West and sees things with clear eyes, he might find a way to cure the curse. Ashitaka resolves to journey to Nago's origin, the lands to the West, to try and find a cure for his curse. He cuts his hair, signifying his permanent departure from his village, and rides out with Yakul, his loyal red elk.

Having traveled some distance, Ashitaka arrives in a forest full of animal gods, including the wolf god Moro. Also in the forest

---
36 Wikipedia: Princess Mononoke. Was available December 2008: http://en.wikipedia.org/wiki/Princess_Mononoke

is Shishigami the Forest Spirit, described as a "god of life and death," that takes the form of a deer during the day and a "night-walker" at night. In his day form, Shishigami resembled a great stag with many antlers and the face of a baboon. He represented Kami in the form of a deer that had tremendous power beyond a human's comprehension. During the night, however, Shishigami became Didarabocchi or the Nightwalker of Kami with gigantic humanoid appearance, a god resembling a human made out of stars with a long pointed face and tentacle-like spikes on the back. He was most vulnerable, however, when he switched from daytime to nighttime and nighttime to daytime. He was greatly feared and revered by the people since he represented the incomprehensible forces of nature. Shishigami was the ancient spirit of the forest who had a number of powers; most notably, the ability to give and take life. Those that Shishigami deemed to live would live; the lives of those Shishigami believed had lived enough, would be taken away. Whenever Shishigami walked in his stag form, plants would instantly come to life at his feet, and just as quickly, they would wither and die. Shishigami gave a kiss to those from whom he took life away and gently nuzzled when giving life to something. [37]

The forest lies beside a human settlement called "Irontown" that clears the forest to get to more iron ore, causing many battles as the animals attempt to protect their forest. It was during one of these battles that the Irontown's leader, Lady Eboshi Gozen, shot Nago.

During the film Ashitaka travels between the forest and Irontown several times, trying to make peace. During Ashitaka's first visit, the village is attacked by San, a human girl who has been adopted by wolves. Ashitaka intervenes to stop the two sides fighting and takes San back to the forest, but is injured in the process. With San's intervention, he is healed of his

---

[37] Princess Mononoke. BeboBC, 2010. Online at http://www.bebo.com/Profile.jsp?MemberId=5355195681

wounds — but not his curse — by the Forest Spirit.

Lady Eboshi learns that the invincible Shishigami became vulnerable when he switches from daytime mode into the Nightwalker. Out of her ignorance she comes to believe that one can control the destructive force of nature by killing Shishigami and so sets out to destroy him. The head of the Forest Spirit is believed to grant immortality; Jigo an opportunistic merchant plans to give the head to the emperor. In return the emperor promises to give Irontown legal protection against the envious daimyos coveting the town's prosperity. [38]

Despite Ashitaka's efforts, Eboshi succeeds in decapitating Shishigami while it is transforming. After Eboshi shoots off his head, Shishigami becomes Didarabocchi, a god of death who resembles God Warrior, a large humanoid made from a dark tar-like liquid in Nausicaä of the Valley of the Wind. Jigo collects the head while the body is transformed into a god of death and tries to run away. Eboshi tries to control the spiritual forces of nature by killing Shishigami, but fails, and creates a disaster. In wrath, Didarabocchi utterly destroys Irontown that Eboshi spent many years to construct. To stop the monster with no head from reaching the villagers, Ashitaka and San take the head from Jigo. By returning the head to the Forest Spirit, the land becomes green again and Ashitaka's curse is finally lifted. [39]

Shinto Motif in Princess Mononoke: Respect for Nature

Just like most other Miyazaki narratives in both films or manga, the underlying theme of *Princess Mononoke* is a continuing battle between natural forces and humanity and a charismatic Chaste Heroine who pursues the possibility

---
38 Princess Mononoke. BeboBC, 2010. Ibid.
39 Princess Mononoke. BeboBC, 2010. Ibid.

to reconcile the two. Thomas P. Kaslis notes that the film eloquently illustrates the theme of Kami associated with the awe-inspiring aspects of Mother Nature.[40] Miyazaki has deliberately chosen the temporal setting for Mononoke and the Muromachi era (1392-1573).[41] Historians describe it as a time of great upheaval when the relationship between humanity and nature was radically changing in Japan.[42] "Hand-cannons" or firearms had been brought in by the Portuguese in 1543 and the Iron Age was dawning. However, Miyazaki is not attempting historical realism in his depiction of the era; rather, he appears to illustrate a power shift in the growing conflict between the natural world and newly industrialized humans. And so, it was the time when humans declared war on the "kamigami," the wild gods. Miyazaki comments:

Japanese did kill shishigami, "Deer God," around the time of the Muromachi era. And then we stopped being in awe of forests - from ancient times up to a certain time in the medieval period, there was a boundary beyond which humans should not enter. Within this boundary was our territory, so we ruled it as the human's world with our rules, but beyond this road, we couldn't do anything even if a crime had been committed since it was no longer the human's world - After shishigami's head was returned, nature regenerated. But it has become a tame, non-frightening forest of the kind we are accustomed to seeing. The Japanese have been remaking the Japanese landscape in this way (1997).[43]

Miyazaki's sympathies lie with the pre-modern world. The two

---

40 Thomas P Kasulis. Shinto — The Way Home (Honolulu, USA: University of Hawaii Press, 2004) p. 76
41 Lucy Wright. Forest Spirits, Giant Insects and World Trees: The Nature Vision of Hayao Miyazaki. Journal of Religion and Popular Culture, 2005.
42 Wikepedia: Princess Mononoke. Online at http://en.wikipedia.org/wiki/Princess_Mononoke
43 Hayao Miyazaki in "An Interview with Hayao Miyazaki," Mononoke-hime Theater Program, July 1997. Edited by Deborah Goldsmith. Online at: www.nausicaa.net/miyazaki/interviews/m_on_mh.html

heroes are both taken from this wild time before the forests were subjugated. Princess Mononoke of the title is modeled on a Jomon period pottery figure, and Ashitaka's people, the Emishi, are suggestive of the Ainu or other groups that, like the forests, were pushed back by the growing Yamato civilization. Linking these two are the markings shared by Hii-Sama and San. They both wear decorative headgear. Even the *Didarabocchi*, the night-time manifestation of the Spirit of the Forest, bears distinctive rope-like marks on its body similar to those that characterized the pottery of the Jomon era. They stand in for the original state of Japan when hunter-gatherer societies lived in relative harmony with nature. Miyazaki stated earlier that he sees the agricultural settlement of Japan as the beginning of the end of the reign of the forest. In an interview on the ecological world of Nausicaä, of the ideas that strongly inform Princess Mononoke, he says, "I was trying to summarize the history of humans since the beginning of farming, in pre-historic times - since we first began to tamper with the world - the existence of humans became complicated with the start of farming."[44] He has also admitted to being heavily influenced by 1970s conservationism and Marxism.

It is not only the respect for kami that Miyazaki uses these characters to represent, they also manifest ideas about a non-intellectual understanding of spirituality that has been divorced from institutionalized religion per se. Miyazaki has depicted the spirits of the forest in various ways - from the shishigami, a gentle giver and taker of life, to the active, violent wolf and boar gods. But he believes his use of the kodama was the most effective. He contends that:

The idea came to me because what I was interested in portraying was a sense of the depth and the mystery, the friendliness and the awe-inspiringness of a forest, and so I came up with the idea of a kodama. I think you can draw all

---
44   Hayao Miyazaki, 1997. Ibid.

the huge, giant trees in the world that you want to. It won't have the same impact. And I wanted to choose a form that represented the liveliness and the freedom and the innocence that a baby represents. And that's why I chose that form.[45]

In a world where magic exists and gods walk the earth, it makes sense for humans to commune with this liminal realm. So, in the Emishi village, Hii-Sama is respected as she consults her divining stones, and her words to Ashitaka are filled with portent: "You cannot change your fate. You can, though, rise to meet it. Go, and see with eyes unclouded." [46] This kind of mystically-oriented intuition has been identified by contemporary Shinto scholar Stuart Picken (2002) as key to Shinto experience:

The sense of the mysterious at the heart of life, the desire to commune with it, and the willingness to express dependence upon it is the root from which all mythological expressions of religious experience spring. The way of the kami thus arose in the Japanese people of ancient times from their reverence for and pre-intellectual awareness of the structures of being that surrounded them.[47]

Lady Eboshi, however, an embodiment of modernism, laughs when Ashitaka relays his purpose "to see with eyes unclouded by hate." She rejects it and through her scorn the pragmatism of modernity rejects the simplicity of primitive spiritual thought in favour of the materialism and rationality privileged by the modern world.

Eboshi, leader of the Irontown or Tatara-ba (whose name is phonetically close to the tatari, or cursed god) and the loci of "modern" ideas, admits she would burn the forest down to get to the iron ore in the mountains, and is prepared to cut the

45 Hayao Miyazaki, 1997. Ibid.
46 Lucy Wright, 2005. Ibid
47 Stuart Picken. Shinto (CA, USA: Stone Bridge Press, 2002)

head off the shishigami to secure a future for her people. She performs this deed, calling to her hunters, "Watch closely. This is how you kill a god."

Nevertheless, Eboshi is not an evil character without good qualities such as caring for lepers, educating women to be more than brothel-workers and building a community in a hostile world. She epitomizes the modern drive that moves towards progress at any cost. Miyazaki has described her as a "contemporary" character:

I conceived of Eboshi as the most contemporary character in Princess Mononoke, and I say "contemporary" and "modern" because she no longer is the slightest bit interested in the salvation of her own soul. She kills off a god with the force of her own will. The monk Jigo is too afraid to do the killing himself, and so he makes others do his dirty work for him.[48]

Eboshi's actions pose the question "Which is more important -humanity's survival or nature's?" Eboshi signifies a break from the pre-modern past as she moves into the non-ritualistic, non-spiritual future. And, importantly, she is not judged for this as her character both has a worthy justification and also learns from the disastrous consequences of her action. Miyazaki admits that "there can be no happy ending to the war between the rampaging forest gods and humanity."

Shinto Archetypes & Princess Mononoke

Hii-sama, one of Miyazaki's most prominent Shamaness archetypes, is described as the custodian of the lore of the Emishi people. She practices their wisdom, passes judgement on Ashitaka and confers ancient rites of burial onto the cursed god Nago. She also conveys wisdom to children, such as when she tells Kaya not to touch Ashitaka's cursed wound.

---
48 Hayao Miyazaki, 1997. Ibid.

Her statements are final, it is she who banishes Ashitaka, and states that he will be dead to his people. Her mastery of ancient divinatory or oracular techniques is fairly comprehensive and competent, she uses runes/stones to correctly determine what Ashitaka must do in order to heal himself and settle the unrest in the Western region in Japan. [49]

Most isolated and wild, Princess Mononoke, whose real name is San, is an almost perfect example of the Chaste Heroine archetype. Unlike Nausicaä and other Miyazaki heroines, she is completely isolated from all human contact, including a human family and friends. She lives in a forest and is so isolated and wild that she isn't considered human – by herself or others. She is a virginal maiden and therefore is so surprised when Ashitaka says 'live, you're beautiful', that she recoils from him, and then threatens to take his life. She possesses the instinct of a wild animal and fights like a beast, and is first seen by Ashitaka sucking the poisoned blood from Moro the wolf-god. She facilitates positive change in herself and others when she is the catalyst for saving Ashitaka's life after he is shot. She communicates very well with the kami, and is a daughter of Moro the wolf kami. She speaks on behalf of the kami when she says to Ashitaka; 'the forest spirit brought you back to life again. He wants you to live.' [50]

Ashitaka can be considered the antithesis of the imperial Yamato warrior, usually concerned with disrespecting the land and conquering on behalf of the Emperor (Tucker, 2003, p. 83). He is ostracized from his Emishi people in the first quarter of the movie and later isolates himself from the people of the iron town. He is only connected with other humans in an emissary capacity. He is a catalyst for the heroine's growth, and defends her from Lady Eboshi, tells her to stop fighting so she may live, and places a blanket over her when she is sleeping. He risks his own life twice to save her

---
49 Moonvoice Ravenari, 2006. Ibid.
50 Nausicaä and other Miyazaki heroines are wild in their own ways and partially isolated from human community, but not completely like San.

life. As a catalyst for her growth, he tells her she is human instead of a beast and makes her aware of her self-ostracism and human beauty. He fights on behalf of the land and kami and defends the forest spirit and forest from Eboshi's iron town. He is also a pacifist, preferring all other routes before resorting to minimalist violence where he prefers to wound instead of kill.

Lady Eboshi from Princess Mononoke is a fascinating character and perhaps the strongest example of the Greedy Magna Mater. She is very concerned with wealth and riches, and triumphantly exults to Ashitaka; 'when the forest has been cleared and the wolves wiped out, this place will be the richest land in the world.' She makes brutal decisions in order to achieve this, from cursing Nago the boar-god and fatally wounding Moro the wolf-god, to desiring to kill the forest spirit. But she also protects and loves the prostitutes whom she has given a good life within the iron town. She has a shelter for lepers, and treats them with care. Osa, a leper, says; 'she's the only one who saw us as human beings. We are lepers, the world hates and fears us, but she took us in and washed our rotting flesh and bandaged us.' She is both kind and harmful to Ashitaka. When Ashitaka blames her for his fatal curse, she says with genuine regret; 'I'm the one he should have put a curse on, not you.'

Despite her good intention and heart of charity, Eboshi was the ultimate loser who tried to control the spiritual forces of nature by killing Shishigami. But she failed and created a tremendous disaster loosing her fortune and one of her arms out of ignorance and naivety.

Moro, the wolf-god/kami, displays little affection towards all humans with the exception of her 'daughter', Princess Mononoke. When first introduced, she is shown attacking and killing humans and livestock and in her last shot where her head is cut off, she bites off Lady Eboshi's arm. Frequently she treats Ashitaka with hostility, despite the fact that he rescued Princess Mononoke. At one point she says to him, 'I was hoping you'd cry out in your sleep, then I would have bitten your head off to silence you.' Yet all her animosity towards humans is grounded in her dislike of their invading her territory, the sacred forest that communes with her. Later, she shares with Ashitaka the truth of why she is so violent towards humans. She teaches life/death cycles, and confers the purpose of the forest spirit to other kami when she says, 'the forest spirit gives life, and takes life away. Life and death are his alone.' She facilitates growth, forces Princess Mononoke to confront Ashitaka's feelings for her, saves her from the cursed boar-god Okkoto, and is a catalyst for the shaping of the new iron town. After the angry Daitarabocchi utterly destroys the village and decapitates Moro's head and bites off Eboshi's arm, it is likely that Ashitaka becomes the new leader of the iron town, though the story does not state one way or the other.

Both Shishigami in *Princess Mononoke* and Ohmu in *Nausicaä of the Valley of the Wind* are described as the Impartial Kami who are often antagonistic against humanity and hated by the Greedy Magna Mater archetypes like Eboshi and Kushana. In contrast with these two, San and Nausicaä are described as the Chaste Heroine who lives in harmony with the nature and Impartial Kami or a guardian spirit of the land. By killing the Impartial Kami, the Greedy Magna Mater often create destructive and demonic Kami like Daitarabocchi, God-Warrior and Kami in the State Shinto and Emperor cult Pre-Second World War Japan. They are nurturing and compassionate persons with good intentions and loyal to their friends, yet fail to produce good fruit because they are too short-sighted and lack the wisdom to set long-term goals.

Philosophical Assumption of Miyazaki Anime: Halfway to the Truth

In almost all Miyazaki's narratives there are two important tenets of Shinto, respecting the kami and love of nature. Miyazaki's films often emphasize environmentalism and the fragile nature of the Earth. He supports environmental conservation expressed through pagan spirituality and Shinto ideals of respect for nature. The influence of Miyazaki's early interest in Marxism is also apparent in some of his films viewing capitalism as a culprit of environmental destruction, although his Shinto based spirituality is incompatible with Marxian dialectical materialism. Some of these works have a strong flavor of traditional Japanese culture and ancient animistic spiritual beliefs. He views that earth's ecosystem is under threat from modernization and industrialization and there is a sense that, like the infinitely accommodating faith of Shinto, there is a position from which the conflict can be resolved. Norinaga maintains that this is achieved not by choosing sides, but by respecting the values of both forces: "Even in the midst of hatred and slaughter, there is still much to live for. Wonderful encounters and beautiful things still exist."[51]

According to Norinaga's philosophy (1764), Kami are not omniscient and transcendent in the Christian or Muslim sense, but exist in a similar way to the Greek gods; capable of human emotion and accessible to mortal communication. In other words, they are not designers of the universe but are created beings in the same level as angels. Shinto does not postulate the existence of the ultimate creator/designer and views that all creations including Kami are the products of an undirected process such as natural selection. The fundamental philosophical assumption of Shinto is that everything in the physical world such as plants, animals,

---
51 Moto-ori Norinaga, 1764. ibid.

rocks, stars and planets as well as spiritual beings similar to Kami and ghosts, exist without a maker. The Kojiki (712 C.E.) details the creation myths of Izanagi and Izanami and events in "the age of the kami," including how the grandson of Amaterasu Omikami, Emperor Jimmu, was set upon the imperial throne. It is a creation story without the creator. Izanagi and Izanami are progenitors of all things who are "procreated," but not "created."

Shinto philosophy is very contrary to the intelligent design theory coming from the Judeo-Christian tradition that holds "certain features of the universe and of living things are best explained by an intelligent cause of a supreme designer".[52] Philosophers have long debated whether the complexity of the universe and natural world indicates the existence of a purposeful natural or supernatural designer/creator(s). Although Miyazaki as a spiritual Avatar of Norinaga, he is aware of the complexity of the natural and supernatural world of this universe and pays deep reverence toward them, he does not admit a purposeful designer or architect who existed from the eternal past and created the universe and all things in it. For me, this sound like Miyazaki and his spiritual mentor Norinaga are half way to the truth.

Because Miyazaki does not postulate a designer of the whole universe, we may view some unrealistic optimism in his works. For instance, though he is deeply aware that humans are culprits destroying the eco-system of the earth and Mother Nature, his philosophy on the redemption and recovery from the defilement of sin is extremely shallow and unrealistic. He believes that the defilement is simply washed away in a bath or spiritual bath house as in Spirited Away. However, Christians have developed a realism or awareness that the bath with simple water is not good enough to remove our defilement, so that we need the Messiah's blood. In Spirited

---

52 Wikepedia: Intelligent design. Was available December 2008: http://en.wikipedia.org/wiki/Intelligent_design

Away, Kamaji the boiler man with six limbs places various formulae in bath water in which their clients bathe. From the Christian viewpoint, none of these formulae works to remove the stain or the ultimate deficit of humanity. According to a legend, Cleopatra of Egypt sacrificed young virgins for the blood bath to sustain her eternal beauty and youth. If we dare to use the analogy of a bath to cleanse our defilement, it must contain the blood of our redeemer instead of virgins as a bath formula.

[53] Hayao Miyazaki. My Neighbor Totoro. Wallpaper manga totoro, 1988/1993.[54]

---

53 Was available May 2009: http://www.annuaire-web-france.com/wallpaper.php?id_wallpaper=1567&tlien=800_600

54 The picture is used under "fair dealing" (Canada) and "fair use" (USA) provisions in copyright law.

3

Space Operas & World of Fantasy by Leiji Matsumoto
(松本 零士)

Leiji Matsumoto is famous for his space operas such as Space Battleship Yamato, Captain Harlock, Queen Millennia, Galaxy Express 999 and Galaxy Railways. Many contemporary (this way you don't need to mention their birth dates, unless they have deceased) experts such as Toshio Okada and Eiichiro Oda have remarked that the romanticism prevalent in his work has inspired them. His style is characterized by tragic heroes and tall, slender, fragile-looking heroines with strong wills and in some cases, god-like powers and a love to mix analog gadgets and the space age.

Matsumoto started his career as an artist under his real name, Akira Matsumoto, in 1953. In the early years of his areer he mostly drew romantic *shōjo (young girl) manga* aimed at a female audience between the ages of 10 and 18, although e intensely disliked this genre. During this period, however, he met his wife, shojo manga artist, Miyako Maki (who's better known as the creator of the doll, Rika-chan, the Japanese equivalent of Barbie). It wasn't until the mid-1960s that he obtained an opportunity to publish in magazines aimed at boys.[55]

---

55 Originally, ronin (浪人, rōnin) refers to a samurai with no lord or master

Matsumoto had his big break with Otoko Oidon in 1971, a series that chronicled the life of a ronin or a young man and woman preparing themselves for entrance exams to universities and colleges. The series was met with both critical and public acclaim. Around the same time he started a series of unconnected short stories set during the Second World War, *Senjo (Battlefield) Manga Series*, which would eventually become the popular anime under the title *The Cockpit* (1993). [56]

Both his involvement in *Space Battleship Yamato* (1974) and the debut of the highly popular series *Captain Harlock* and *Galaxy Express 999*. both in 1977, made him one of the most popular artists in the entire manga-industry. In 1978, he was awarded the *Shogakukan Manga Award for shōnen* (award for boys' manga) for *Galaxy Express 999* and the *Second World War Battlefield Manga Series*. The animated versions of *Captain Harlock* and Galaxy Express 999 (1978) proved to be very successful. Both series are based on the same universe sharing several crossover characters. These produced several spin offs and related series, most notably *Queen Emeraldas* and *Queen Millennia*. This shared universe is often called the *Leijiverse* or the *Matsumoto Milieu*. [57]

By the late 80s, Matsumoto's influence faded. However, the introduction of an all-new Galaxy Express 999 series in 1998 was greeted with a great success and started a "renaissance" era of Leijiverse. Since then numerous anime based on his works have been produced, including *Captain Harlock OVA*, as well as several animations based on *Maeter* the protagonist

---

during the feudal period (1185-1868) of Japan. A samurai became masterless from the ruin or fall of his master, or after the loss of his master's favor or privilege. The term is also used in modern Japan for students who have failed the yearly school entrance examination for the high school or university of their choice, and then decide to spend the next year studying to retake the exam.

56 Leiji Matsumoto (Wiki) http://en.wikipedia.org/wiki/Leiji_Matsumoto
57 Leiji Matsumoto, ibid.

of Galaxy Express 999 and other aspects of the Leijiverse.[58] Leiji Matsumoto is also often mistakenly credited as the sole creator of Space Battleship Yamato (known outside Japan under various names, but most commonly as *Star Blazers*). He was, however, brought onto the project after its conception by producer Yoshinobu Nishizaki. But it is now generally agreed that Matsumoto's artistic vision and direction is the primary reason Yamato had such a memorable success. Matsumoto created a manga loosely based on the series, and the Yamato makes brief appearances in several of his works including the Galaxy Express 999 manga. A recent work by Matsumoto originally named *Great Yamato* (2001) featuring an updated Yamato had to be renamed *Great Galaxy* due to the legal issues with Nishizaki. As of this writing, both Matsumoto and Nishizaki are working on independent anime projects featuring the acclaimed Space Battleship Yamato, with the conditions that Matsumoto cannot use the name Yamato or the plot or characters from the original and Nishizaki cannot use the conceptual art, character or ship designs of the original.

Yamato the Space Opera

Space Battleship Yamato (宇宙戦艦ヤマト Uchū Senkan Yamato) is a Japanese science fiction anime series and the name of its historical space craft. It is also known to English-speaking audiences as *Space Cruiser Yamato* or *Star Blazers*. An English-dubbed and partly edited version of the series was broadcast on American and Australian television under the title *Star Blazers*.

Conceived in 1973 by producer Yoshinobu Nishizaki, the project underwent heavy revisions. Originally intended to be an outer-space variation on *Lord of the Flies*, the project at first was titled *Asteroid Ship Icarus* and had a multinational teenage crew journeying through space in a hollowed-out asteroid in search of the planet Iscandar. There was to be much discord among the crew; many of them acting purely out of

---

58 Leiji Matsumoto, ibid.

self-interest and for personal gain. The enemy aliens were originally called *Rajendora*.

When Leiji Matsumoto was brought onto the project, many of these concepts were discarded. It is his art direction, ship designs and unique style that accredit him in fans' eyes as the true creator of Space Battleship Yamato, even though Nishizaki retains legal rights to the work.

First Season - Space Battleship Yamato (宇宙戦艦ヤマト)

The first season began airing in Japan in 1974. The first season contained 26 episodes, following Yamato's year-long voyage out of the Milky Way Galaxy and back again. As the story continues, it features the declining health of the determined *Captain Okita* (Avatar in the Star Blazers version), and the transformation of the young orphaned teenager *Susumu Kodai* (Derek Wildstar) into a mature and capable captain, as well as his budding romance with female crewmember *Yuki Mori* (Nova). In the climax, Yamato goes to the Large Magellanic Cloud leaving the Milky Way Galaxy. Then, he lands the Iscandar, after confronting and destroying the Gamilas civilization. Yamato's crew then meets Queen Starsha and Susumu's lost brother Mamoru.

Captain Mamoru Kodai of the Starship Yukikaze was once captured by the Gamilas, but escaped while being transported to their home world and landing on Iscandar. When Susumu met Mamoru, he discovered that his brother and Stasha were deeply in love. The planet Iscandar was a beautiful Class M planet while her sister planet Gamilas was a non-class M planet. Queen Starsha is a beautiful female humanoid that looks almost identical to humans and requires a Class-M atmosphere. It is intriguing that Class-M planet humanoids live side by side with Non Class-M planet residents and are sometimes in love with each other. We can conjecture that the relationship between humans and the imaginary residents of Mars could be similar to the one between residents between Gamilas and Iscandar.

Yamato leaves Iscandar and returns to earth before nuclear radiation kills all humans. Yamato has one more battle with Desslar in which Yamato destroys Desslar's home world. Desslar's palace is launched as a spaceship with a similar capability as Yamato. His battleship is equipped with a warp engine and *Deslar Canon,* or wave motion gun with Gamilas technology. However, Yamato's chief science officer Sanada has developed a device to create deflector shields. As Dessler shoots at Yamato with his Desslar Canon, Sanada uses his deflector device against Desslar. Then, the massive tachyon energy[59] force from Desslar's starship is deflected, he goes back to his own and destroys the ship instantaneously.[60] Desslar seems to be dead when his battleship explodes. However, he comes back in the later stories. Captain Okita dies shortly before the end of the successful mission to bring back the device Cosmo DNA from the planet Iscandar.

In 1978 Westchester Corporation identified Yamato as a potential "kids' property," and bought the rights to the first two seasons. The company produced *US TV Series - Star Blazers* or a US version of Yamato edited and dubbed into English. Dubbing and editing were done by *Griffin-Bacal Advertising* and production and syndication by *Claster Television*. Being marketed at a school-age audience, the content was largely recreated by the American editors in order to satisfy the broadcast standards and practices offices of American TV stations.

In the Star Blazers, the ship is still the historical Yamato, but

---

[59] A tachyon (from the Greek ταχυόνιον, takhyónion, from ταχύς, takhýs, i.e. swift, fast) is any hypothetical particle that travels faster-than-light.

[60] Wikepedia: Tachyon. Was available December 2008: http://en.wikipedia.org/wiki/Tacion

is renamed the *Argo* once rebuilt. Principal changes included Westernization of character names as well as ship's name, reduction of personal violence, toning down of offensive language and alcohol use, and removal of sexual content and references to the Second World War although the sunken battleship ruins were still identified as the Yamato in dialogue.

The very Japanese theme of "the honorable enemy" was also a important aspect of Desslok's (Desslar) character development in the second and third seasons, as well as in the later movies.

Movie - Arrivederci Yamato
(さらば宇宙戦艦ヤマト 愛の戦士たち)

In 1978, Yoshinobu Nishizaki decided that it was time to end the old Yamato saga and produce the movie *Arrivederci Yamato* or *Farewell to Space Battleship Yamato*. This film 'terminated' most of the original Yamato cast and became popular enough that fans demanded a sequel. This film was later reworked into a second TV season that became known as 'Yamato 2'.

In *Arrivederci Yamato*, the Yamato and her crew face the onslaught of the Comet Empire, a civilization from the Andromeda Galaxy who seek to conquer Earth, led by Zwordar the Great (Prince Zordar). The Earth ship is aided by a woman made of anti-matter, Teresa of Telezart (known as Trelaina in the English dub), while the Comet Empire has restored to life Earth's greatest enemy, the Gamilas' leader Desslar, who is eager for revenge. After a massive battle which destroys both Earth and Comet Empire forces, the Yamato crew defeat Zwordar's plans, but at the cost of the ship and their lives.

Desslar, the nemesis of earth humans, reappears in this series. After his battleship is destroyed, he is cast out and drifts in space. The spaceship of the Comet Empire finds him and brings him back to life because Emperor Zordar finds him useful. Because the Comet Empire makes Desslar a cyborg as they resuscitate him; he obtains the capability to survive in Class-M atmosphere. He appears in the same location as Susumu Kodai without a helmet. In the movie, Desslar dies as well as most of the Starforce. As Desslar dies, being defeated in the battle with Yamato's crew, the movie uses his theme song, praising him as an honorable rival of the Starforce and "samurai with blue skin" from outer space.

At the end, Susumu Kodai (Derek Wildstar), sits beside a dead Yuki (Nova) and teams up with Teresa of Telezart (Trelaina) to succeed in crushing the Yamato into Zordar's gigantic battleship that is the same size as the moon, saving Earth but killing himself in the process.

The end of this film received attention from the critics and provoked controversy. Many Japanese as well as Americans, Chinese and Koreans found it a disturbing film because Susume Kodai, the protagonist, saves the earth in the same way the Kamikaza pilots did during the Second World War. It is also the same method as Mohamed Atta (1968-2001,) the Al-Qaeda Warrior, took control of American Airlines Flight 11, the first plane to strike the World Trade Center on September 11, 2001. It is believed that the end of the story in which Susumu saves the earth at the expense of his life was mainly Nishizaki's idea, and Matsumoto later expressed regret that the ending romanticized a quasi-Kamikaze or Al-Qaeda style suicide bombing.

The most significant difference between the movie version and the TV version lies in the fact that the subsequently produced TV version spares the lives of most of the cast, contrary to the original ending of *Arrivederci Yamato* movie.

Second Season - Space Battleship Yamato 2
(宇宙戦艦ヤマト2)

This is a TV series with the same story setting as the movie *Arrivederci Yamato* (さらば宇宙戦艦ヤマト 愛の戦士たち) (also rendered as *Farewell to Space Battleship Yamato*). As the popularity of this series grew due largely to an enraged fan outcry from those who saw the movie *Arrivederci Yamato*, a second season of the television series was produced, presenting a different plot against the movie's enemy without killing off the Yamato or its primary characters. Expanding the story to 26 episodes, the second season features additional plots such as a love story between Teresa and a Yamato crew member Daisuke Shima (Mark Venture), and onboard antagonism between Kodai and Saito (Knox), leader of a group of space marines. Teresa is not an anti-matter woman but an ordinary female Class-M humanoid with power to control anti-matter. So Shima had no difficulty to be in company with her. The English dub of this season is considered the best by many of the series' American fans. Some footage from *Arrivederci Yamato* was reused in the second season, particularly in the opening titles; the sequence of the Yamato launching from water was also reused in two of the subsequent movies. However, the entire story was largely modified.

Yamato: The New Voyage
(宇宙戦艦ヤマト 新たなる旅立ち)
(The television movie Yamato)

The New Voyage came next, featuring a new enemy, the Black Nebula Empire. The year is 2201, and in the aftermath of a harrowing battle with the Comet Empire, the Yamato is forced to take on new crew members in the third chapter of the continuing chronicles of the Space Battleship Yamato.

In this film, Desslar sees his homeworld destroyed by the

grey-skinned aliens, its twin planet Iscandar being next in line for invasion. He finds an eventual ally in the Yamato, on a training mission under acting captain Kodai.

Following some theatre and TV movies, a third season of the TV series was produced, broadcast on Japanese television in 1980. The film deals with the Sun being hit by a missile that greatly accelerates nuclear fusion activity and rapidly ages the sun. Because of this, humanity must evacuate the earth or prevent the sun from becoming red giant star and eventually going supernova. In this series, there is an appearance of a significant human character that is not Japanese. He is an American astronomer who discovered an abnormality of the sun that greatly accelerated nuclear fusion.

Other Yamato series
The theatrical movie *Be Forever Yamato*

*(*ヤマトよ永遠に – 1980) sees the Black Nebula launch a powerful weapon at Earth that will annihilate humanity if they resist a full-scale invasion. The Yamato, under a new captain, travels to the aliens' home galaxy, only to discover what appears to be a future Earth in which terrible future events have come to pass. The anime series continues the saga of the Yamato crew's battle with the aliens of the Black Nebula Empire. Blasting off in an attempt to reach the attackers' homeworld, the ship passes through the Black Nebula only to discover that they have actually warped 200 years into the future, a point in time when the Earth has been defeated. Refusing to surrender, the crew embarks on a mission to travel back through time in an attempt to change history. The saga ended in 1983 with the fifth film, *Final Yamato* (宇宙戦艦ヤマト 完結編 – 1983).

In this feature, the Gamilan Empire is destroyed by a chance collision of galaxies, while the Yamato, back under the command of Captain Okita (who was cryogenically frozen after his apparent death in the first season), encounters the planet Deingil too late to save its humanoid civilization from being flooded by the water planet Aquarius. The surviving Deingili, a warrior race who believe only the strong should survive, plan to use Aquarius to flood Earth and destroy humanity, in order to create a new home for their race. When all seems lost, the Deingili are destroyed by Desslar and the remains of his people (in gratitude for the human crew's having honored the Gamilan dead earlier in the film), and the Yamato is filled with purified water and detonated like a giant hydrogen bomb by Okita to divert the water stream. A great deal of time is taken at the end of the film showing the fragments of the Yamato repeatedly "sinking" beneath the waves in space, Okita going down with his ship.

In the mid 1990s, Nishizaki attempted to create a sequel to Yamato, set hundreds of years after the original. *Yamato 2520* (ヤマト 2 5 2 0) was to chronicle the adventures of the eighteenth starship to bear the name, and its battle against the Seiren Federation. Much of the continuity established in the original series (including the destruction of Earth's moon) is ignored in this sequel. In place of Leiji Matsumoto, American artist Syd Mead (b. 1933) provided the conceptual art.

Due to the bankruptcy of Nishizaki's company *Office Academy*, and legal disputes with Matsumoto over the ownership of the Yamato copyrights, the series was never finished and only three episodes were produced. Most Yamato fans were generally underwhelmed by the series' first episodes and were not disappointed by its cancellation.

In March of 2002, a Tokyo court ruled that Nishizaki legally owned the Yamato copyrights. The two parties eventually settled, and Nishizaki began work on a new movie titled Yamato Rebirth (set after the original series), while Matsumoto planned a new Yamato series. However, additional legal conflicts have aborted both projects.

Possibly Inspired by Matsumoto Anime - USS Yamato in StarTrek

In *the Star Trek: The Next Generation* (1987–1994), there was an appearance of a Galaxy-class Federation starship named USS Yamato (NCC-71807). In one TNG episode titled *Contagion*, a fake and unmanned reproduction of the lost starship USS Yamato is created by Nagilum to test the crew of the USS Enterprise. D. Lieutenant Worf, who was familiar with the Yamato's internal layout and Commander Riker, investigates the reproduction before it is erased by Nagilum.
Later that year, the actual Yamato, under the command of Captain Donald Varley, was destroyed with all hands while in the Romulan Neutral Zone. An Iconian software transmission had caused an antimatter containment failure. The magnetic seals around the dilithium chamber collapsed, and the computer initiated its emergency release system to dump the Yamato's supply of antimatter. However, the virus caused the release to halt with antimatter remaining within the ship, resulting in a warp core breach.

According to technical illustrator and modeler Rick Sternbach (1991)[61], Yamato's name is after the historical battleship Yamato, that served with the Imperial Japanese Navy during the Second World War. He said the name is not a deliberate reference to the Japanese anime series Space Battleship Yamato (or Star Blazers in North America), even though he and several other members of the production staff are fans of Japanese animation. It is easy to speculate that he denied the reference to the anime so that Star Trek producers could avoid prompting the controversy as to "who stole what". USS Yamato was easily destroyed by a Romulan battleship because it was not equipped with the powerful Wave Motion Gun. We can easily speculate that perhaps Sternbach made this statement to safeguard the StarTrek from potential copyright

---
61 Wikia Entertainment: USS Yamato: Was available November, 2008: http://memory-alpha.org/en/wiki/USS_Yamato

related troubles with Nishizaki. He could be aware of the legal trouble between Nishizaki and Matsumoto, although the conflict between the two was not revealed in public when STNG was produced. We can also ask the following question. It is easy to speculate that if USS Yamato was not destroyed by Romulans and appeared in STNG and other StarTrek series several times, or the producers even created a new series *StarTrek: Yamato*, Nishizaki would go after the StarTrek for copyright infringement.

Yamato & Nationalist Worldview of Matsumoto & Nishizaki

It is generally believed that the end of the story of Arrivederci Yamato, in which Susumu saves the earth with Kamikaze or Al-Qaeda style suicide bombing, is primarily Nishizaki's idea. According to Tomohiro Machiyama (2008), however, Matsumoto was at least partially responsible for the nationalistic side of this work.[62] He stated that in Matsumoto's Senjo or Battlefield Manga Series, the heroes are always Japanese or Germans. On the other hands, Americans are depicted as stupid, weak, cruel, ugly and cold-blooded racists. Machiyama also pointed out some ethnocentric aspects of Yamato stories, saying that:

Contrary to the multiethnic crews of StarTrek, the Yamato's crew is all-Japanese. It's not just that there are no non-Japanese earthlings shown during the whole Yamato saga. Other countries have already been annihilated by Gamilus. And the final hope of the earth is Yamato, a restored WWII battleship that was the final hope of Japan in 1945 (2008).

In Star Blazers, or an English-dubbed and partly edited version, names of all crew members are given English names. If the viewer is watching only this version, he or she will not see

---
62 Tomohiro Machiyama. The Birth of a Nation. Otaku USA. February, 2008.

the darker nationalistic side of the author. However, in the original Japanese series, all human characters except one American astronomist in the *Third Season - Space Battleship Yamato III*, had Japanese names. The leadership of the Earth government did not believe in his findings of the abnormality of the sun's nuclear fusion, because he was a country bumpkin from America.

We can safely assume that Matsumoto views Japan as an elite nation among the Earth Humans. Machiyama continues to argue that Japanese call their spirit "Yamato Damashii" and the ultimate deed of this spirit is the Kamikaze attack. Yamato seems to be a powerful symbol of "Japaneseness" that resides within the collective unconscious realm of the nation, and in Matsumoto's space drama, she went up to space or the heavenly realm.

Machiyama stated that Yamato's Kamikaze style attack was Nishizaki's idea, and Matsumoto was reportedly disgusted at it. However, he admitted that the very ending of the movie *Arrivederci Yamato* was completely consistent with Matsumoto's Yamato theme. Thus, there is no reason that we can put the entire blame on Nishizaki as the solo culprit for the pro militarist ending of the movie.

Yamato & Mishima

While Matsumoto seems to be promoting the Japanese patriotism and ethnic elitism that many Japanese might hold in their unconscious, in Yamato and Battlefield Manga Series, Nishizaki had a necrophiliac tendency to romanticize the death for great causes, possibly inspired by Yukio Mishima (1925–1970), a Japanese author, poet and playwright.

Mishima's short novel Yūkoku, or Patriotism (1960), is based a historical event that took place February 26, 1936.

Lt. Takeyama is the main character, a member of a terrorist group who attempted to overturn the Japanese government. It depicts the love between him and his wife Reiko[63]. Takeyama is a naval officer who supports an attempted coup, but is barred by his fellow officers and friends from participating in it because of his wife Reiko. When the coup fails, Takeyama is given the order to execute his comrades. Takeyama contemplates harakiri, or taking his own life, due to his loyalty to his friends, but that will make Reiko a lonely widow. The couple decides to commit suicide together, with Takeyama going first. In the movie Arrivederci Yamato 's last scene, Susumu Kodai vows the eternal marriage oath in the afterlife to the dead Yuki sitting beside him, shortly before he teams up with Teresa of Telezart and crashes into Zordar's gigantic battleship. This shows a very strong link with the patriotic theme in Mishima's Yūkoku.

In 1970, Mishima himself visited the Tokyo headquarter of Japan's Self-Defense Forces and committed a ritual suicide with the form of *Harakiri*. It was his way of protesting against Japan's post-Second World War democracy and the new constitution after the war.

Apart from Nishizaki, Matsumoto does not have the appearance of Mishima's necrophiliac influence, because he does not romanticize the death *per se*. Since all Yamato series are collaborations between Matsumoto and Nishizaki, many major characters like Mamoru Kodai, Stasha, Sasha and all Yamato's captains die likely because of Nishizaki's idea. Death of these characters seems to be consistent with Mishima's philosophy that the death for a greater good is the ultimate accomplishment of one's life. Matsumoto also seems to have abstained from the expression of his nationalistic worldview in creating most other space dramas.

---

63 Yukio Mishima. Patriotism. (NY: New Directions Publishing Corporation, 1960/1995)

Space Pirate Captain Harlock
TV Series

In the original television series (1978), Harlock's crew included the mysterious, alien woman Miime, who consumes alcohol as her staple diet, a robot, and a drunken doctor who resembles Dr. Sado of Yamato. The series presents a story in which a huge black metal sphere strikes Tokyo by an alien race named Mazone. These Modigliani-necked Floronic humanoids with plant-based bodies explored Earth in the mythic past and are now back to reclaim it. Only Harlock and his mismatched crew are brave and capable enough to confront the enemy.

Directed by Rintaro (b. 1941), the series features some innovative directing stunts, such as split screen and flashbacks, excellently served by a symphonic score of the *Tokyo Philharmonic*. Some of the mechanical design on the series strongly resembles the first Star Wars film prompting some controversy as to "who stole what". [64]

Character of Captain Harlock

Captain Harlock and his world continued to be developed and occasionally re-developed as Matsumoto changes his conceptions about them. The original Captain Harlock TV series was conceived as an independent, standalone work. Captain Harlock, the space pirate, displays the full range of human emotions at one point or another during the course of the story.

In the sequel TV series to the Arcadia of My Youth feature film, Harlock's back story is significantly changed. He is a military officer, captain of the starship Deathshadow before he becomes a space pirate. Harlock as an ex-military officer may

---
64 Captain Harlock (Wiki) http://en.wikipedia.org/wiki/Captain_Harlock

have followed the idea from Manga version of Yamato that he was formally Mamoru Kodai, the captain of a military ship.

This series also has a completely new story setting in which Harlock was married. The tragic death of his wife Maya at the hands of Earth's alien conquerors plays a large part in turning Harlock from defeated space soldier to brooding space pirate. The backgrounds of other major characters, such as fellow pirate Emeraldas and best friend Tochrio Oyama, were also altered in accordance with Harlock's new backstory.

When Matsumoto's works again became popular in the 1990s and he began to pen the Harlock Saga manga, he changed the backdrop of Harlock and his universe. It is also said that Matsumoto incorporated *Wagner's Ring Cycle* into his work and made significant reworking of almost every one of Matsumoto's stock stable of characters in order to make the story fit. One example is that Harlock is only a teenager when the Earth is conquered and his father Great Harlock is the first to take up the "fight for freedom" touched upon in Arcadia of My Youth. As of 2007, this is the version of Harlock that Matsumoto considers in continuity. Harlock's appearance in *Space Symphony Maetel* tries to consolidate previous adaptations of the character.

Other Appearances

Captain Harlock has made frequent cameo appearances in many other works of Leiji Matsumoto, including Yamato, Galaxy Express 999, Queen Emeraldas, and Galaxy Railways as a kind of joker in a deck of playing cards.

In the Manga version of Space Battleship Yamato, Harlock was the second identity of Mamoru Kodai, brother of Susumu Kodai and former captain of the lost starship Yukikaze. Captain Harlock as Mamoru Kodai was originally intended to appear in the TV version of Space Battleship Yamato during their return voyage from Iscandar. The idea was dropped for a number of reasons which likely included the fact that the rights to Yamato were at the time owned by executive producer Yoshinobu Nishizaki. This idea evolved into simply finding Mamoru Kodai (Alex Wildstar) alive on Iscandar. The idea was still used later in a Yamato manga by Matsumoto where Yamato later encounters Mamoru who assumed the secret identity of Captain Harlock. Some manga versions even mixes two ideas and Harlock as Mamoru is romantically involved with Stasha.

The most recent significant appearance of Harlock is in *Cosmo Warrior Zero* (2001). In this story the main character is Captain Zero. Harlock, Tochiro and Emeraldas put in mostly supporting guest appearances, and are shown as slightly younger than their previous incarnations. Harlock, who is significantly younger than his appearances in the previous movies, doesn't yet have his trademark eyepatch. It might indicate these incidents took place in his earlier days before he lost one of his eyes in a battle.

Most notable is the return of Harlock's ship to the original Blue Arcadia Design (not seen since the original TV series). Though now green and named Deathshadow, the name of Harlock's first battleship when he was still a military officer, the design is altogether different. In Yamato Manga, Harlock as Mamoru Kodai appeared as the captain of the pirate ship Deathshadow. In the film "My Youth in Arcadia" in 1982, he was the captain of the ship with the same name before becoming a pirate who later built the new starship Arcadia.

The setting of this movie is the 30th century when humanity is reaching as far as Andromeda, several centuries after the time of *My Youth in Arcadia*, although Harlock and other characters are younger. It indicates that in *Cosmo Warrior*

Zero, the continuity is essentially nonexistent as is usual in most other Matsumoto anime. Harlock and others appear as if coming from an alternative universe with different histories even though the series features story points appearing in previous Matsumoto films and TV shows. Alternatively, we can view the Harlock of this series as a descendent of the one in *My Youth in Arcadia* and *999*, because this character appears in various eras in Matsumoto's anime and manga including the *Battlefield Manga Series* dealing with Second World War.[65]

My Youth in Arcadia & Productions after 2000

The film *My Youth in Arcadia*, (1982) set in a different continuity from the original TV series, chronicles Harlock's youth in the spaceship Arcadia. The film features a newly designed starship and lacks most of the crew from the Space Pirate series, but is noteworthy for the presence of Emeraldas, a female counterpart to Harlock originally appearing in a series of Matsumoto-penned graphic novels.

December of 2002 saw the release of the movie *Captain Herlock: The Endless Odyssey*, directed by Rintaro. Originally meant as a TV series, delays to the production caused it to be released only on video. Matsumoto initially cancelled the Endless Odyssey series due to the use of the Star of David as the demonic aliens' symbol.

The story follows the original TV series. Although nearly every part of this series is a sequel to the original *Captain Harlock, Endless Odyssey* reintroduces Tadashi Daiba to the Arcadia. The redheaded Mazone spy Shizuka Namino also reappears, now as a black-haired holographic assistant to Dr. Daiba, and the date of the series is approximately 100 years after the original series. The question remains - did Harlock and his

---

65 Harlock who is in *My Youth in Arcadia* and Galaxy Express 999 is Harlock VIII, in eighth generation from Phantom F. Harlock who lived in the 19th century. The one who appears in the *Battlefield Manga Series* is Harlock II, son of Phantom.

crew become cyborgs or immortal by eating some elixir? Also, is Matsumoto a forerunner of postmodernism shown by the fact he made the setting in this way to demonstrate the degree to which he disdains full and logical continuity?

The answer to the first question would be "no," since Matsumoto anime does not carry the theme of immortality. Therefore, he never creates immortal human characters although some alien characters are either complete immortals or near immortals with extremely long lifespan. However, it is highly likely that the answer to the second question is true. Matsumoto anime was post-modernistic even in the late 1970s when it demonstrated the philosophy that time is relative. Some of Matsumoto characters have time travels although travelling into the past or future is not his main focus. In his narratives, time is not always linear and sequential and often streams backward. In Galaxy Express 999 manga, there is a brief cameo appearance of Yamato when the train encounters the "time knot" in which two different times are overlapped, so that the passengers of the space train sees Yamato from the past.[66] Because time is not linear and sequential, it also allows a character to have multiplicity in the past. Captain Harlock is descended from German pilot Phantom F. Harlock in one reality. He was once, however, Mamoru Kodai, the captain of the lost starship Yukikaze, in some other reality. Matsumoto allows his characters to shift realities back and forth in his universe.

Crew of the Arcadia

Tadashi Daiba is the audience surrogate, the viewer's gateway to Harlock's world, and plays almost the same role as the wandering sailor Ishmael in *Moby-Dick* (1851) by Herman Melville. The character of Harlock is described from the viewpoint of Daiba in the same way as Ishmael describes Captain

[66] The time setting of Galaxy Express 999 is few centuries after the one of Yamato.

Ahab on a whaleship. Daiba was probably named after Daiba Datta, a disciple and one of the cousins of the historical Gautama Buddha (563 BC to 483 BC) of India. Tadashi is sometimes in conflict with Harlock early in the series, but he would become a trusted part of Harlock's senior staff as the series progressed.

Doctor Zero is Arcadia's Chief Medical Officer and is a very humorously drawn character who likes to drink sake during his medical practice in the same way as Yamato's Dr. Sado. He has a pet cat called Mi-kun, which also appears in Space Battleship Yamato as Doctor Sado's cat. Mi-kun also makes on-off appearances in several other anime such as Queen Millennia and Galaxy Express 999.

The Mazone

The Mazone are the major villains of the original 1978 series. They belong to the intelligent plant-based species in primarily female human form but with a few in male form. As the race is basically asexual like plants, their apparent gender, however, is superficial rather than functional. When a Mazone dies, the corpse spontaneously burns to ashes. Shizuka Namino is a Mazone spy posing as the Earth Prime Minister's secretary. She attempts to assassinate the Prime Minister and set Commander Mitsuru Kiruta up to take the blame for the deed. Then she releases Kiruta from prison and attempts to seek sanctuary on the Arcadia, with the intent of sabotaging the ship from the inside. Harlock discovers Shizuka's origins and Shizuka finds she is unable to return to the Mazone caravan, but she shows admiration for Harlock's noble actions to take her aboard by forcing him to kill her rather than face certain death at the Mazones' hands. The character of Shizuka would later return in the 2002 Endless Odyssey OVA series as the holographic assistant of Professor Daiba.

Galaxy Express 999

Galaxy Express 999 (銀河鉄道999, Ginga Tetsudō Surī Nain) came into the existence as a manga written and drawn by Leiji Matsumoto in 1977, and birthed various anime films and a TV series. The manga won the Shogakukan Manga Award for shōnen in 1978 and the anime series won the Animage Anime Grand Prix prize in 1981. A striking and unusual feature of this series is that trains are going to space and travelling to distant planets and galaxies.

Original storyline – Manga & TV Series
(you're back to just storylines)

The story of Galaxy Express 999 (1978) is set in a space age, high-tech future, where cyborg people with "machine bodies" are pushing humanity with organic flesh and blood towards irrelevance and extinction. A young boy named Tetsuro Hoshino desperately wants an immortal and indestructible machine body, giving him the ability to live forever. Tetsuro learns that while machine bodies are extremely expensive, they are understood to be given away for free on a planet in Andromeda Galaxy, the end of the line for the space train Galaxy Express 999. Technology has advanced to the point such that space-faring vehicles can assume any shape, such as the steam locomotive in the story.

Characters from other Matsumoto works appear in GE999, notably Captain Harlock and Emeraldas with a brief appearance by Yamato. In later stories, there is an appearance of a mysterious machine man named Faust who wears a outfit similar to that of Darth Vadar in Star Wars. Faust is an old friend of Harlock, the long lost father of Tetsuro.

Movie Version

The movie version of Galaxy Express 999 (1979) is nearly identical to the original story in terms of plot, but with much more condensed storyline. Rather than visiting over 100 different planets as Tetsuro and Maetel do in the original manga/TV series, they only visit four. Some of the most popular characters like *Antares, Claire, Emeraldes* and *Captain Harlock* make brief appearances. Also, rather than kill Count Mecha on Earth, Tetsuro confronts him in the *Time Castle* on *the Planet Heavy Melder*.

Adieu Galaxy Express 999

Adieu Galaxy Express 999 (1981) was a sequel to the movie version. *Adieu* follows an entirely new storyline that takes place two years after the destruction of the planet Andromeda. The machine empire becomes stronger and more controlling of the Galaxy. Rumors abound that Maetel is the new Queen Prometheum. Tetsuro, a freedom fighter, is shocked when a messenger brings him news that the 999 is returning. Tetsuro narrowly makes his way to the 999 and departs Earth. As the 999 departs La Metal, Maetel finally makes her appearance.

The 999 continues on to the planet Mosaic, the last stop before Great Andromeda Station and the capital of the machine empire. Tetsuro is almost killed when he finds the Ghost Train. The 999 finally arrives at Great Andromeda station where Faust greets Tetsuro once more. Meanwhile, Maetel travels down to the center of the planet where her mother Queen Prometheum's spirit still exists. Maetel is put in charge of the mechanized empire and she reveals that the energy force the machine people use for their survival is actually drained from living human beings. About this time a great comet, Siren the Witch, approaches Great Andromeda, sucking up all machine energy. With Great Andromeda collapsing, the 999 is set to depart, but Tetsuro must face Faust one last time. At the end Tetsuro learns that Faust is actually Tetsuro's long lost father. The 999 heads back to La Metal where Maetel and Tetsuro separate once more.

Queen Millennia

As one of Leiji Matsumoto's moderately well-known works, the Queen Millennia series was broadcast as a TV show in 1980 -1981, and followed by at least one manga. The movie was released in 1982, adapted from the 1981 Japanese animated TV series of the same name. In manga and the TV series, Yayoi/Queen Millenium, the main character, was a waitress in a ramen restaurant with a mysterious secret identity. However, in the movie, her day time identity was a schoolteacher and part-time lab assistant.

TV Series - Queen Millennia

In *Queen Millennia* (新竹取物1000年女王, Shin Taketori Monogatari Sennen Joou), the 1980 TV series begins with the adventures of a young boy named Amamori Hajime who gets involved in a bizarre struggle between two planets. At the beginning, Hajime meets a Yayoi Yukino (Millenial Queen).[67] She is from Lar Metal, a wondering planet that drifts through space without orbit, home to a far more advanced civilization than the earth.[68] Every 1,000 years, Lar Metal passes close to Earth, bringing chaos and disaster to humanity. During this time, one of the Lar Metal females comes to Earth to see her home land until the time when it will come again in 1,000 years. Lar Metal residents also have extremely long life spans

---

67 Yayoi's last name "Yukino" means "snow-field." Her true name is Andromeda Prometheum and it suggests a linkage with other stories in Leijiverse.
68 Planet La Metal also appears in Galaxy Express 999 and the evil queen who is mother of Maetel and rules two galaxies is also Promethium. However, there is no likelifood that Yayoi the Queen Millennia is not Metal's mother, although these two are supposedly related. Also, the name "La Metal" has association with "ramen" noodle or Matsumoto's most favored food.

and 1,000 years for them is equivalent to only one year for humans.

Lar Metal is to pass closes to Earth on September 9, 1999 and the day is getting close. For humanity, it might bring near-apocalyptic destruction. Meanwhile, Yayoi begins a course of her own, one which only she knows. She can no longer stand idly by and watch her home land destroyed.

Her full name is Queen La Andromeda Prometheum, the same name as the mother of Maetel and Emeraldes. The other Prometheum gets her body mechanized by a crazed cyborg scientist who turns her into an evil queen with a machine body who rules the Andromeda and Milky Way galaxies in the story of Galaxy Express 999.

Summarizing the story of Queen Millennia, many of the characters in Queen Millennia bear resemblance and some linkage to characters in Galaxy Express 999, so viewers may speculate how those characters in the two stories relate each other. Although there is little likelihood that Yayoi is the identical person as Metal's mother, some imaginative anime fans may create a story that Yayoi turns into a cyborg later in her life and tragically transformed into an evil character. However, Yayoi who belongs to an immortal race does not seem to require a cyborg body to live forever.

Movie - Queen Millennia

Queen Millennia is a two-hour feature film created by Leiji Matsumoto based on the 1981 Japanese animated TV series of the same name. The movie retells the story told in the 42-episode series that deals with the disastrous approach to Earth of La Metal, the home planet of the Millennia Queen. Yayoi Yukino, who has been living life as a school teacher and part-time lab assistant, is shocked to discover that her fellow

La Metallians have secret plans to displace all humanity on Earth. Previous queens included historically existing female monarchies like *Himiko* from Japan, *Yang Kwei Fei* from China and *Cleopatra* from Egypt. The story states they all loved the earth, lived long and died after millenniums of life.

Yayoi resolves to fight back and defend her beloved Earth and humans, with the help of her astronomer boss, Professor Amamori, and his nephew, Hajime. The invasion team also includes Yayoi's La Metallian partners, her sister Selene and her male assistant, Yamori. The most complicating matter is the fact that the La Metallian invasion fleet is commanded by Yayoi's home planet boyfriend, Fara. The climax is set for a huge interplanetary battle, with the Earthmen relying on Yukino's massive underground ship, the "Ark," that emerges from the ground just in time to confront the La Metallian forces.

As in so many Leiji Matsumoto works, the extraordinary events are revealed largely through the eyes of a young boy, in this case Hajime, Dr. Amamori's nephew. He is traumatized early on in the story by the death of his parents in an explosion related to the manufacture of parts for the Queen's Ark. As an amateur astronomer and one of Yayoi's adoring students, he is slightly more sophisticated than Tetsuro of "Galaxy Express 999," a poor boy in shabby cloak and battered hat.

The movie features a rich, evocative music soundtrack by New Age composer Kitaro. There are some memorable wordless musical sequences, such as one showing the people of La Metal slowly emerging from their 1,000-year sleep and awakening to embrace each other and enjoy the "Spring" on their strangely colorless planet. Another sequence has Hajime being shown aboard the underground Ark and led down a very long corridor housing the dead former millennial queens. Later in the story, three of these queens, all famous figures from different countries' lores, Himiko (Japan), Yang Kwei Fei (China) and Cleopatra (Egypt), come to life to aid Yayoi when a woman whose body is made of flaming fire sacrifices her life. At the end, Yayoi loses her life to protect earth's humanity and all La Metallians went back to a hibernation as their planet moved away from the Sun.

The last scene is emotionally moving, excellently done and exquisitely designed, considered one of the masterpieces that emerged from the pen of Leiji Matsumoto. The impressive end song is sung in English by Dara Sedaka, daughter of American pop star Neil Sedaka.

The Galaxy Railways

The Galaxy Railways (銀河鉄道物語 Ginga Tetsudō Monogatari) is a 26-episode sci-fi anime series about flying trains set in space. This series has the same striking theme as its predecessor Galaxy Express 999 in which trains are going up to space and travelling to distant planets or even galaxies. The English version was broadcast on American TV beginning Monday, June 19, 2006.

In 2006, a sequel series, *The Galaxy Railways: Ginga Tetsudō Monogatari Eien e no Bunkiten* (銀河鉄道物語 -- 永遠への分岐点,) translated into "Crossroads to Eternity" in English began broadcasting in Japan for a projected 26-episode run. Also, there is a 4-part OVA series *Ginga Tetsudō Monogatari ~Wasurerareta Toki no Wakusei* (銀河鉄道物語 --忘れられた時の惑星) translated into "The Galaxy Railways: Planet of Forgotten Time" in English.

Synopsis

The fleet of the Galaxy Railways transports countless galactic passengers, both humans and aliens, from one planet to the next, protected by the *Space Defense Force*, or SDF, the elite force protecting the Railways Fleet against space pirates, terrorists, meteor storms and antagonistic aliens.

SDF, with heavily armed space trains, holds even space fighter planes inside similar to conventional aircraft carriers in order to uphold the reputation of maintaining the best transportation schedules within the Universe. They are to deal with accidents, natural disasters, rescue operations and defending the trains from enemies.

In the beginning of the story, the main character, Manabu Yūki, has always had dreams of joining the SDF from his childhood, following in the footsteps of his father and brother, who died in the line of duty while serving in the SDF. Unfortunately, his mother who runs a Ramen restaurant, is tired of losing her and does what she can to deter him from following his dream. Despite this, Manabu boards the train to Destiny Station. There, he is assigned to the team boarding the Big One, being led by Schwanhelt Bulge, an officer once serving under Manabu's late father.

Shortly after joining SDF as a young man of 20, Manabu experiences a "time slip" which sends him five years into the past to encounter his dead brother Mamoru during a crucial battle with space pirates. He told Mamoru that he came from the future to fight the enemy side by side. Manabu went back to his time leaving his brother behind, because taking Mamoru out of his time to save him from the impending death is against the rules of SDF and considered as interference with the past.

Layla Destiny Shura is a mysterious beauty unifying SDF and all lines on The Galaxy Railways. She also knew Manabu's arrival long time before it happened. She possesses the ability to see the destiny of planets, human beings and living things.

Despite being a "Guardian of Destiny", she is unable to tell passengers what difficulties lay ahead of them. But an appearance of those who use evil powers to change the destinies of these travelers triggers another of her hidden abilities.

Unlike Yamato series in which almost all important earth humans are Japanese, the SDF soldiers of this series are more multi-cultural with a good number of both Japanese and Westerners and some artificial lifeforms like Yuki the android. However, unlike Startrek Universe, the SDF does not include members of alien species except Layla Destiny Shura the Supreme Comander of the whole military division of the Galaxy Railways.

Yuki is a medical android called "sexaroid" who is assigned to the Sirius Platoon. In Matsumoto anime and manga, "sexaroid" is a female android. The name sexaroid implies a certain job function as a comfort woman for Japanese Imperial Army performed during the Second World War, though that never comes into play with Yuki as she is instead programmed to be the unit doctor.

Apart from Yuki, most conductors seem to be artificial. They have a similar appearance to the *conductor* of the space train 999, with a machine body. However, there is a crucial difference between the 999's conductor and other conductors in Galaxy Railways. The conductor of the 999 whom Tetsuro encountered is a cyborg that used to have an organic body. On the other hand, the conductors of the later series are constructed as androids, and their personalities are programmed by men. They are pure machines with no organic past to be either human or alien. Also, most cyborg people possess a higher social status than organic people with flesh and blood, because they are wealthy enough to purchase very pricy mechanical bodies. On the other hand, android workers of the Galaxy Railways are treated as properties and expendable tools without civil rights.

Story

The story begins on Destiny station, which claims to be the center of the Universe, where all the terminals of "The Galaxy Railways" are gathered. The main character, 20-year old Yuuki Manabu, carrying on his dead father and brother's will, joins SDF to protect the safety of the Railways.

Manabu is assigned a commission with the Sirius Platoon, his father's old party, on the rebuilt Big One under Captain Bulge, his father's old first officer. With his placement, Manabu worked hard to prove that he belongs in the SDF, and though he often disobeys orders to do what he thinks is right and disciplined as the consequence, he quickly gains a reputation throughout the force as a great soldier.

The majority of this series consists of the day-to-day battles of an SDF platoon. The SDF is in charge of ensuring that The Galaxy Railways run smoothly. Their jobs range from assisting a train that has broken down to combatting terrorists hijacking and bombing trains or situations.

Manabu also has a great deal of respect for Captain Bulge who always seems to make the correct decisions and never gets too critical of Manabu for following his feelings. Bulge had been the first officer for Manabu's father, and he was the man that carried the news of Wataru's death to the Yuuki family.

Another crew member who joined up with Sirius Platoon at the same time as Manabu is Louis Fort Drake. Manabu meets her on the train heading to Destiny Station from his home planet. The relationship between the two develops throughout the series, and Louis is the first member of the SDF that Manabu meets when he is officially accepted, and it is also her that Manabu goes to most often when in trouble or needing help.

Spiritual Dimemsion of Matsumoto's Space Opera

Clark H. Pinnock states that the popularity of science fiction and their extraterrestrial settings might be an indication that people look for God in outer space. Pinnock contends that because God reveals his glory in the universe, man is inclined to look at space (1980).[69] The marvel and mystery of the universe is one of the greatest parts of God's revelation. Chinese Taoism holds the Jade Emperor, the ruler of heavenly realm, as well as other deities, in space. Contemporary horoscope culture also holds that constellations of stars are modeled after Greek mythology as deities in space who might determine people's destinies. Although original Greek mythology does not view its deities as living in space, the horoscope culture transfers them to the world of stars or constellations.

Matsumoto's space dramas are based on the assumption that deities and spirits reside in outer space, and people go to space in order to get closer to the spiritual world. Viewing and studying Matsumoto anime closely, one can easily conclude that although he does not believe in one creator of the universe, he is greatly moved and inspired by the greatness of God's creation and looks for the divine and spiritual components of the universe.

The backbone of *Galaxy Railways* has a theme of a popular culture of horoscope and Platoons of Space Defense Force (SDF) are named after the alpha stars of several major constellations like Sirius Platoon and Vega Platoon. The horoscope views that the stars determine the destiny of people and the rail is a symbol of destiny and fate.

Matsumoto and his predecessor Miyazawa took a train to space despite how unrealistic and technologically challenging

---
69 Clark H Pinnock. Reason Enough. (Burlington,Ontario: Welch Publishing Company, (1980)

it appears, likely because the train can serve as a symbol of the pilgrimage of life. The train is a better symbol of the life journey than the starship because it must follow the rail, the symbol of rules one must follow. Likewise, stations symbolize events that we encounter in various stages of life.

Galaxy Express 999 has some similarities to the American Wild West movie, and nearly every episode brings Tetsuro and Maetre, two main characters, to a new planet and new people and new lessons and observations on humanity. Some planets and their people are shallow and selfish; others are unpleasant but decent at heart; some are full of despair; some are full of life and laughter. They are caricatures of human nature, often emphasizing the extremes that can result if people let their vices (or virtues) hold sway.

Tomohiro Machiyama stated that Matsumoto has an obsession to place anachronistic machines in deep space, such as the steam train in Galaxy Express 999, the pirate sail ship in Captain Harlock and the Second World War battleship in *Yamato*.[70] Taking a steam train or conventional diesel or electric train to space and using them as intergalactic transportation might mean an even larger technological challenge than converting an old pirate or Second World War battleship into a starship with warp capability. The idea of a train running in space seems ingenious and fascinating, yet it is not Matsumoto's original idea. The setting of a steam train going to space is apparently inspired by *Night on the Galactic Railroad* (銀河鉄道の夜, "Ginga Tetsudō no Yoru" – 1937), a children's story by Kenji Miyazawa (1896 - 1933).

The railroad is also a symbol of man's destiny and fate that many believe cannot change. The theme of railroad as the destiny is more prominent in the Galaxy Railways than the Galaxy Express 999, and the home base of SDF (Space

---
70 Tomohiro Machiyama. The Birth of a Nation. Otaku USA. February, 2008.

Defense Force) is located in the symbolic Destiny Station. Also, Layla Destiny Shura, the supreme commander of SDF is also described as the woman who possesses the ability to see the destiny of planets, human beings and living things. The story does not give us her clear identity, whether she is a human or alien or some kind of deity. Viewers, however, may consider her a goddess in heaven who administers all destinies of theuniverse. Another speculation may be that Layla belongs to the same race as Maetel or Millennia Queen, an alien species with supernatural powers.

At the same time, Matsumoto also boldly postulates an existential theme on man's free will over destiny and fate to choose his or her own life. While the railroad in space might be a symbol of our destiny, the pirate ship of Captain Harlock is a symbol of our free will. Among all *Leijiverse* characters, Harlock is most heroic because he is constantly fighting fate and destiny around him with his powerful personality. Yamato's crews are heroes within a limited domain, in a society or community with a certain cause and ideology. Susumu Kodai was as heroic as members of a Kamikaze party who crashed into American battle ships and Mohamed Atta of Al-Qaeda who set a course of hijacked passengers in a plane into the World Trade Center.

In the Galaxy Express 999, Matsumoto also displays the underlying philosophical assumption to value mortality over immortality and free will rather than fixed destiny. Tetsuro finds that among all mechanical people, Crystal Claire, who works aboard 999, has a tragic life. Her body, always nude, is a beautiful clear crystal, yet she longs for the warmth of a human touch. Unlike others who gave up their humanity by choice, Claire's statement strongly indicates that she was forced into the cyborg body against her will by her mother. Claire may symbolize people who are forced into a certain life or vocation by their own parents. She could represent anyone who fails to choose his or her own school, career, spouse, and direction in life because of the toxic interference of parents. This person may feel like a machine with no real life like Claire because her parents blocked the healthy development of ego identity with sense of autonomy and self responsibility. Claire may symbolize typical upper middle class Japanese woman during the era in which Matsumoto grew up, who allow parents to make all major decisions in their lives.

However, they are not heroes outside of their ideological communities. Likewise, for average citizens of the Comet Empire, Susumu Kodai is a notorious terrorist and extremely shady character similar to Osama bin Laden. On the other hand, Harlock is an archetype of the universal hero with his own autonomy and free will to fight his his destiny. He does not belong to any nation-state, or a community governed by ideologies, but is completely his own. He often fights with aliens to protect earth and humanity.

The water planet Aquarius of the *Final Yamato* also seemingly conceives a horoscope theme. Particularly, Aquarius is often equated with post-modernity led by *New Age Spirituality*. If Yamato is as a powerful symbol of Japaneseness or "Yamato Damashii," then the ending that she is sinking to the water of planet Aquarius, a symbol of post-modernity in which all ethnicity and nation-states are devolving into one global community, must be a more realistic conclusion. The beginning of the era of Aquarius or the age of globalism and post-modernity is indeed the end of nationalism, patriotism and ethnocentric Yamato Damashii.

The story of *Millennia Queen* is roughly based on Kaguya-hime (かぐや姫, "Princess Kaguya"), the principal character in Japanese mythology Taketori Monogatari (竹取物語) or *The Tale of the Bamboo Cutter*[71]. The story states that she

---

[71] The Japanese title of the *Millennia Queen* is *Shin Taketori Monogatari Sennen Joou* (新竹取物語 1000年女王) or "New Tale of the Bamboo Cutter - Queen Millennia."

is from Tsuki-no-Miyako "The Capital of the Moon," being found in the form of a female human baby with unusual radiance from her body. This baby girl, discovered by a childless bamboo cutter, grows up quickly and becomes a beautiful young girl at the same pace as Sasha in Yamato. The bamboo cutter and his wife name her Kaguya-hime or "Princess Kaguya," and raise her as their daughter. Many men including the Emperor of Japan fall in love with her. However, she declines all offers, saying she is not of this world. She stays in contact with the Emperor, but continues to rebuff his requests to marry, although she was in favour of him and appreciates his friendship. She finally returns to the moon or the world she came from when her time on the earth ends and a heavenly troop ascends to take her back. As the Emperor learns the day of Kaguya's return is approaching, he sets many guards around her house to protect her from the Moon troop who have come to get her. But when a vehicle of "Heavenly Beings" arrives at the door of her foster parents' house, the Imperial guards are blinded and disarmed by a strange light. Shortly before she leaves Earth, Kaguya writes sad notes of apology to her parents and to the Emperor. Then she takes a small taste of the elixir of life that might give the Emperor immortality, attaches it to her letter, and gives it to a guard. The guard returns it to the Emperor with the items Kaguya-hime had given him as her last mortal act.

The Emperor reads her letter and is overcome with sadness and decides to burn the letter at the top of Mount Fuji, the highest mountain of Japan. He does it with the hope that his message will reach the distant princess sending a message that he does not desire to live forever without being able to see her. Possibly, she wanted to see him after several thousand years, therefore she wanted him alive by the time of reunion. She might have another chance to visit the earth. However, the Emperor was too desperate and short sighted to understand Kaguya's true intention.

The plot of the *Millennia Queen* that Yang Kwei Fei of China and Cleopatra of Egypt lived thousands of years seems ridiculous by historical standards. If both of them have a La Metallian lifespan, they would be still alive in the 21st century. But Himiko of Japan is a more obscure character than the other two and has more room for imaginative stories. In fact, there is little historical account about her life, and the dates of her birth and death remain mystery. Some even argue that she did not exist.

Although Leiji Matsumoto does not seem to have a good comprehension of Christianity, the story of *Millennia Queen* is loosely linked with the biblical theme of the Millennium Kingdom, in which Jesus Christ rules 1,000 years. In Matsumoto's story, queens who arrive from the Planet La Metalle replace the role of Christ. Matsumoto secularized and relativized the concept of the Millennium. Matsumoto named the secret starship of the Millennial Queen hidden in underground - "Ark," probably because he had some knowledge of Noah's Ark constructed during the pre-historic era. The end song composed by an American, indicates a more biblically oriented worldview than Matsumoto. The song says that Yayoi is a lovely "Angel Queen" who has floated down from the sky. It sounds as if she is one of angels sent by the true God instead of a queen from the planet La Metal.

Matsumoto initially cancelled the Endless Odyssey (2002) series due to the use of the Star of David as the demonic aliens' symbol, since he was reportedly horrified and made the following statement: "My blood was frozen when I found the Star of David symbol .... I believe you cannot debase any religion...I bear that in mind whenever I make stories. I cannot allow my characters to appear in any anime that tramples on my philosophy."

This might indicate that he pays some respect to Judaism and

Christianity. However, the symbol that Rintaro intended to use as the symbol of an evil empire was likely the Pentagram, not the Star of David. The Pentagram is often used as a symbol of pagan mysticism, occult and Satanism in the West and as the two are extremely similar. The chances are high that Rintaro and Matsumoto's staff, with little or no knowledge about Western occult and Satanic cults, mixed up the two symbols.

Leiji Matsumoto. Otaku USA. Herndon: VA, June 2009.[72]

---

[72] The picture is used under "fair dealing" (Canada) and "fair use" (USA) provisions in copyright law.

All pictures in this book are used under
"fair dealing" (Canada) and
"fair use" (USA) provisions in copyright law.

Cover Anime Artist: David Sivertsen
All Rights Reserved
dave.longquan@gmail.com

4

Dynamic Mythological World of Go Nagai
(永井 豪)

Part 1 - Demons & Spiritual World of Go Nagai

Go Nagai (永井 豪 Nagai Gō, born Kiyoshi Nagai, September 6, 1945 in Wajima, Ishikawa), is a Japanese manga artist and important innovator of several genres within anime and manga. Impressed by the Mangas of Tezuka Osamu, decided to be a cartoonist himself. Nagai developed the concept of giant robots transforming ('Mazinger and Grendizer), an idea that has been used in numerous television series. He was born on Sep. 6th 1945 in Wajima city, Ishikawa pref. After graduating from Itabashi High School of Tokyo, Nagai wrote and failed the entrance exam of the Waseda University each year during the next three years. He also had a major health problem and suffered a severe case of non-stop diarrhea for 3 weeks. He finally gave up his plan to go to prestigious Waseda University coming to the conclusion of becoming a manga artist and doing something that he liked as a child. Nagai became an assistant of Ishimori Shotaro and started his life as a professional cartoonist. After five years and a couple of manga released under Ishimori's tutelage, Nagai decided to strike out on his own. After he had established himself as a manga artist, Nagai industrialized his production by setting up his own company *Go Nagai's Dynamic Productions*. It employed more than 30 assistants. In 1972, Go Nagai started his most famous work, Devilman. Also created in the same year was Mazinger Z. Both titles went on to become anime series later in the year due to their enormous success. Mazinger Z also started the super-robot trend that dominated the 1970's. In the mid-80's, Go Nagai decided the time was right to jump back into the anime world and show the public what he really enjoyed doing with anime.

Ken Ishikawa, who was one of the employees of the company Go Nagai's Dynamic Productions, served as his assistant on many projects. Ishikawa helped Nagai get both his manga and anime career off the ground by starting up animation studios. Later, Ishikawa went on to make manga on his own and established himself, producing works like *Fatal Fury*, *Miroku* and *Samurai Spirits*. His art style is very similar to Go Nagai's although much less gratuitous with nudity.[73]

Nagai created the Mazinger Z (マジンガーZ) series, later expanded into Great Mazinger, Grendizer, and - many years later - Mazinkaiser, where he developed the concept of giant mecha. Mazinger was the first manga in which a giant robot was piloted by the hero, thus creating one of the biggest staples of the industry. Mazinger is considered the first successful "Super Robot" anime show, and has spawned numerous imitations.

Simultaneously to Mazinger, he created one of his most popular manga, Devilman (デビルマンDebiruman), about a demonic hero fighting against hordes of demons. Nagai

---

73 GoNagai (Wiki) http://en.wikipedia.org/wiki/Go_Nagai

also turned Devilman into a series which was less violent and dark than the manga. Years later Nagai revamped this popular series by introducing the main character as a female and altering the storyline. This series is called Devilman Lady or Devil Lady in the U.S. It was first released as a manga and then later as an anime. Go Nagai considers the Devilman series and the Mazinger series, as being his life's work due to their massive popularity all over the world. His fascination with the world of fallen angels in Devilman seemed to have stemmed from an influence from Yasutaka Tsutsui who had a Christian education in Doshisha. He also exhibited a strong interest in Greco Roman mythology in the Western mythology of Mazinger Z.

The manga and anime of Devilman and the spinoff stories stemmed from it are one of most popular and well known creations of Nagai. The Devilman series are embodiments of Nagai's fascination with the demonic, spiritual or supernatural world. He worked with Yasutaka Tsutsui who was educated in Doshisha University a Christian university founded by an ex-samurai Christian educator named Niijima Jō. It is easy to assume that Nagai had a great influence and inspiration from Tsutsui.

Devilman

Devilman (1972, TV series) is the title of a popular manga and anime created by Go Nagai, as well as the name of the main character of the manga and anime. Devilman began as a manga in Kodansha's Shonen Magazine and a 39-episode anime TV series in 1972, and has since spawned numerous other anime, manga and film spinoffs. The manga and anime versions of Devilman series have developed different and distinct story lines as well as characters. Then, Nagai and his producers have created Original Video Animation (OVA), the third version different from manga and TV anime series after 1990s.[74]

74 Devilman (Wiki) http://en.wikipedia.org/wiki/Devilman

Story (Manga)

A long time ago, the Earth was ruled by beings called "demons." The demons constantly fought each other for survival, but soon found themselves fighting a new race of beings: the first humans. The demons then became imprisoned in ice after a great cataclysm. They would remain there until the ice melted, after which it was said Satan would rise and lead them in Armageddon. The protagonist of the story is a teenager named Akira Fudo who later becomes the hero Devilman by merging himself with a very powerful demon named Amon. At first, Akira is a very modest, gentle and somehow timid teenage boy avoiding any conflict. When his parents are lost on a business trip in Antarctica, Akira goes to stay with his childhood friend Miki Makimura. Both soon form a close relationship as the story progresses. Miki, a tough, smart, self-sufficient girl, loves Akira but wishes that he would stand up for himself when he gets pushed around, and is frustrated by his lack of backbone. She often has to defend herself from bullies even when Akira is with her.

One day, Akira's best friend, Ryo Asuka, asks a favor and completely changes Akira's life. Ryo's father had discovered the existence of demons when he found a mask during an excavation of the ruins of an ancient Mayan temple. This mask turned out to be a fossilized demon skull that showed whoever wore it what the world was like when demons ruled over it. Ryo shows Akira the previous world ruled by demons and informs him about the revival of these creatures. Akira then sees Ryo's plan: "To fight a demon, one must become a demon."

Demons have the ability to possess and control humans. Ryo, however, believes that Akira may be able to harness a demon's powers when possessed, due to the fact that Akira has a pure heart. Ryo takes Akira to a nightclub and picks a fight to draw demonic attention to the club. His ploy succeeds: Demons possess the clubbers and threaten Ryo and Akira, until he is possessed by Amon. The Amon is the Lord of War, also called the Beast of Hell, one of the strongest demons. His possession of Akira causes Akira to transform into Devilman. Devilman contains the strength and power of the demon Amon, as well as the heart and soul of the human Akira Fudo, giving Akira complete control. After he becomes Devilman, Akira is no longer timid and shy and becomes very aggressive and no longer lets anyone push him around.

This change pleases Miki who was tired of protecting him from bullies and weak character of Akira that was constantly pushed around. She welcomes Akira's newly acquired transformation, manliness and assertive character. Miki, however, has no idea that some of attributes of Akira's new character are stemmed from the merger with Amon[75] the Lord of the War, one of very powerful angels who rebelled against the Most High following Lucifer even before the beginning of the human history. Although she is unaware of the origin of his newfound powers, she often has to step in to stop Akira when his temper gets out of control.

Throughout the manga and TV anime, Devilman has many battles with the demon hordes. He encounters many foes such as Silene the demon bird (she was also Amon's lover before he possessed Akira), the water demon Geruma, a large turtle-like demon called Jinmen, Zenon who is basically Satan's right hand, and one of the strongest demons, Psycho Jenny, Lala and Saylos.[76]

The story ends with Akira discovering that his friend Ryo is

---

75 Wikepedia: Amon (demon). Was available January 2009:
http://en.wikipedia.org/wiki/Amon_(demon)

76 Lala is a demon in the TV series who transformed herself into a beautiful young woman and attempted, unsuccessfully, to seduce Akira, and Saylos is one of the main villains in the movie Amon: Apocalypse of Devilman.

really Satan in a dormant state. After Miki and her whole family are brutally slain by a paranoid human horde (in a particularly famous scene, Akira retrieves Miki's dismembered body from her burned house and later is seen holding her head in his arms), the final fight between Devilman and Satan ensues. The Earth is totally destroyed during this battle, and Devilman dies at the hands of Satan. Satan regrets what he has done, and then creates the Slumking to punish him for what he did to his beloved Akira. The conclusion leads into a related series Violence Jack in which the story revealed that Jack is no other than the next life of Akira after his battle with Lucifer.

The TV Anime Series of Devilman

Devilman evolved from Go Nagai's previous manga, Demon Lord Dante (魔王ダンテ Maō Dante), after Toei Animation approached Nagai about turning Dante into a television series. The TV producers wanted certain grotesque and violent elements toned down, and a more human-like anti-hero created. Devilman was born as a result of this; Go Nagai worked on the anime's scenario along with Masaki Tsuji, a well-known anime scenario writer and a highly successful and regarded novelist of several mystery fictions. Along with the television series, Devilman was also produced as a serialized manga in Shukan Shonen Magazine over 53 issues beginning in 1972. Go Nagai designed the manga to be more of a horror-like genre and mature than the anime version. It was later reprinted in a five-volume series, and has enjoyed over a dozen reprints and in five different languages. The manga's extreme violence and complex story line made it an instant hit.

The anime series was 39 episodes long and ran from July 1972 to March 1973 on NET (now TV Asahi). The series sported some differences from the manga and the character of Ryo Asuka wasn't created until Go started working on the manga after he finished working on the anime, but was still very popular. Both the anime and the manga also vary on the ending; while the anime series had a bittersweet open-ended finale, the manga had a tragic ending. A decade after the broadcast in Japan, Devilman TV anime went overseas. Rather surprisingly, given its level of violence, the Devilman TV series was also broadcast on TV in Italy in 1983 where Dante's Divine Comedy originated, and also became extremely popular there. The appearance of Devilman was significantly different although they have nearly identical faces. In TV anime, he had no tail unlike the manga version and had a slight resemblance with Batman. In contrast with the anime Devilman who is clothed with a costume similar to Batman, manga Devilman is essentially nude and the lower part of his body is covered with hair like a beast.

OVAs

Two OVAs were released in 1987 and 1990. The late Kazuo Komatsubara (1943 - 2000), an animation director on the original TV series, returned for the OVAs as character designer. The videos revolve around Akira's transformation into Devilman up until his battle with Silene. The OVAs are well animated and, other than a few minor alterations, are faithful to the original manga, as he has tail and no clothes. They were released in the US. during the mid 1990s on video by L.A. Hero, and in the UK and Australia by Manga Entertainment. Manga Video in the USA picked up Devilman after L.A. Hero's licence expired in America. The OVAs remain the only Devilman anime to have been commercially released in the United States.

Iso in 2000, Amon: Apocalypse of Devilman was released as a pay-per-view event in Japan and later released on video and DVD. Perhaps the most violent of all the anime incarnations of the franchise, it covers the period between the humans becoming aware of demons and the final battle between Devilman and Satan. However, in this version, rather than battling Satan, Akira is forced to face his literal "inner demon", Amon, in the final battle. The death of Miki drives Akira to the edge and he loses his hold on Amon, allowing the demon to finally posses his body fully. Amon kills Saylos, the main antagonist of the film. But Akira (surprisingly, still as Devilman) revives and mentally battles Amon for his soul. Just as it seems Amon is about to win, Miki visits Akira in a vision, silently expressing her forgiveness of his failing to protect her. This encounter gives Akira the strength to truly kill Amon and claim the demon's power as his own. Although Akira encounters Asuka Ryo (both are consciously aware of his being Satan), who is, in part, willfully responsible for Miki's death, Akira doesn't battle him in the film, and instead walks past him silently. The conflict between them is left unresolved, thus ending the film. OVA Devilman has also spawned a video game for PlayStation, but none of these games have been released in North America.[77]

Anime, Film and Manga Spinoffs

Many other manga titles were created later on including Shin Devilman (which replaced the entire third volume of the original manga in later editions), Neo Devilman and Amon: The Darkside of the Devilman. Several other books have been published dedicated to Devilman over the last 35 years.

In 2004, a tokusatsu Devilman movie directed by Hiroyuki Nasu using CGI effects was released. Unfortunately, it was generally rejected in Japan, even by Devilman fans. As a consequence, it won Grand Prize in Japan's Bunshun Kiichigo Awards (the Japanese version of the Razzie Awards, which are given to the worst movie of the year).

---

77 Apocalypse of Devilman (2010) http://devilman420.tripod.com/id7.html

Go Nagai also released a manga series called Violence Jack. The series takes place during the aftermath of Armageddon and the battle between Satan and Devilman. In CB Chara Go Nagai World,[78] an online discussion site, it is revealed that Jack is Devilman. This series became an OVA anime in 1986, and was released in the U. S. sometime during the 1990s in an edited version by Manga Video and an uncensored release by Critical Mass. The cast of Devilman, including Akira, Miki, Ryo Asuka, and Silene, also crossed over with characters from Mazinger Z and Violence Jack. In this OVA series released in 1991 it is revealed that Violence Jack is a future version of Akira Fudo.

Popular Reception and Themes

The rich story line in Devilman, in the opinion of several readers of manga, made it stand apart from other manga of the time. Its extreme violence, however, made it a major target of protest for the PTA (parents and teachers association) and other groups. Still, the story has become a classic in Japan and has even been working its way through the U. S. over the past decade or so. The manga has been translated into English in a series of five bilingual manga volumes published by Kodansha, although the only piece of Devilman anime to have been commercially released in America is the two-part late 1980s OVA.

Interestingly, Go Nagai is said to have been highly shocked that his giant-robot work Mazinger Z, which was on Japanese TV at the same time as Devilman and which he originally did not take very seriously, far surpassed Devilman in popularity. The reason for his surprise was was that he had worked especially hard on Devilman and only made Mazinger as a way to "blow off steam."

---

78 CB Chara Go Nagai World. Was available January 2009:
http://www.crunchyroll.com/library/CB_Chara_Go_Nagai_World_OVA?src=trail

In an essay written three decades after the debut of the original manga and TV series, Nagai commented that he designed Devilman as an anti-war work. According to Nagai, the fusion of humans and demons is an analogy for the draft, and Miki's gruesome death parallels the death of peace. "There is no justice in war, any war," wrote Nagai, "nor is there any justification for human beings killing one another. Devilman carries a message of warning, as we step toward a bright future."[79]

Probably Nagai's most well-known and philosophically deep creation is Devilman. Telling the story of Akira Fudo and how he joined with the demon Amon, a Duke of Hell, to protect mankind from legions of demons, Devilman was a breath of fresh air for the industry in that Go refused to censor his ideas. Bloody and brutal demons fighting led to constant clashes with various parents groups, but despite the uproar, the manga proved so popular that an anime was created that same year and ran 39 episodes before finishing in 1973. Devilman, which in a poll after 2005 was picked by the Japanese public as one of their most beloved anime characters, is continued to this day in the *Violence Jack* sequels, *Devil Lady* spin-off and the occasional Devilman OVA.

Many critics argue that the main theme of Devilman is anti-war. Demons fighting were bound to be a bloody and brutal affair, and Go drew it as a symbol of the gruesome reality of wars. When humans transform into devils and demons, what they really are doing is taking up murder weapons and embarking on war. The 'indiscriminate melding of demons with humans' that we see in Devilman refers to the draft system. There is no justice in war, any war, nor is there any justification for human beings killing one another. Devilman carries a message of warning, as we step toward a bright future."[80]

---

79 See: http://www.devilworld.org/revelations.html.
80 See: http://www.animeacademy.com/profile_nagai_go.php

Devilman and Milton's Paradise Lost

The character of Ryo Asuka was apparently modeled after Lucifer in Milton's Paradise Lost. A popular image of Satan, adapted from the Greek God Pan, is a horned, hoofed goat-like monster holding a trident. In modern times, the goat-like image of Satan has been adapted into a more human-looking form of a dark, foreboding man wearing a goatee. Satan has also been depicted as a charming and attractive man, as symbolic of the popular mythology that Satan acquires human souls by appealing to their vanity and presenting them with appealing and attractive temptations. Satan has also been depicted less frequently as a conniving woman, such as in the movie Bedazzled (2000).

Modern and late Medieval Christian thought derived from the interpretation that Lucifer is a fallen angel who is Satan, the embodiment of evil and an enemy of God. In Christian literature and legend, Lucifer is generally considered to have been a prominent seraph in heaven, although some sources (Book of Ezekiel 28:14) say he was cherub and an archangel who had been motivated by pride to lead a revolution against God, in "The War of Heaven." Isaiah 14:12 describes him as *heosphoros* or "dawn-bearer" son of the morning who was cast out of heaven, along with a third of the heavenly host, and came to reside in the world.

There are also a few images depicting Satan as a beautiful angel, such as in Go Nagai's Devilman. Nagai depicted Son of the Morning as a beautiful hermaphroditic Seraphim angel with twelve wings and both penis and breasts. Nagai described Devilman in his manga version as modeled after the Greek God Pan that many Mediaeval painters described as Lucifer. In the TV version, however, he remodeled the appearance to that of a stereotypical anime hero, that somehow resembled the American hero Batman. Devilman's former self was

Amon in which some authors described as one of a third of the heavenly host who followed Lucifer, having the title of prince and forty legions of demons under his command. He is the seventh of the 72 Goetic demons and one of Astaroth's assistants for whom he governs forty infernal legions.

In the story of OVA, Akira and Ryo describe what they have seen in the demon artifact, and the possibility of demons still existing on Earth. Akira thought that mankind was lucky that demons died out before humans were created, but Ryo pointed the impossibility that mankind could have known of demons through legends if they did not exist in their time. Ryo then tells Akira about Dante's "Divine Comedy" where Dante described Hell, Purgatory and Heaven. Ryo goes on and tells Akira of how Dante saw Lucifer, the bat-winged ruler of all demons trapped in ice, locked in motionless torture. Akira then thought that maybe Lucifer was trapped in ice during the Ice Age and that maybe Dante really did see this demon. When telling that to Akira, Ryo had no awareness about his true identity as Lucifer, because he had erased his own past memory when he took a human self as a school boy determined to fight and kill all demons. He says that while mankind is unaware of the demons' existence, demons will sneak from the shadows and kill all of mankind.

Devilman as Post-modern Faust

The story of Johann Wolfgang von Goethe's Faust (1725) concerns the fate of Faust in his quest for the true essence of life. He attracts the attention of the Devil (represented by Mephistopheles), with whom Faust makes a deal to serve him until the moment that Faust attains the zenith of human happiness, at which point Mephistopheles may take his soul. Goethe's Faust is pleased with the deal, as he believes the moment will never come. In the mediaeval Europe, making any deal with demons was taboo and considers a highway to the Hades. He disregards the taboo, however, and makes a deal with the devil Mephistopheles so that he might gain a power to meet his goals. His predecessor in the Tragical History of Doctor Faustus (1604) written by Marlowe, is taken into the underworld immediately after a 25 year trial period in which he enjoys the power and privilege endowed by the hell angel. But Goethe's Faust is shrewder than the older one so that he doesn't allow the devil to set the deadline in which his soul is taken. Instead, he makes a deal that his soul would be taken into the Hades for one moment in order for him to experience a single moment of happiness.

Likewise, Akira Fudo chooses a union with Amon to gain power over other dark angels, having abandoned humanity. The devil Mephistopheles tries to grab Faust's soul when he dies but fails, is frustrated as the Lord intervenes – recognizing the value of Faust's unending striving. In Devilman, Ryo or Lucifer himself approachs Akira and introduces him to Amon, or a demon like Mephistopheles. However, Amon who takes over Akira's body with the intention to merge and assimilate his human soul into the demon's self fails to do so. Instead, as Akira's human self completely takes control over Amon's demon body and self, the demonic power is completely subjugated under Akira's humanity. The motif that Akira takes over Amon's body as a weapon to fight against Lucifer's army is an extension of the Faust theme and follows the philosophy of eye for eye, tooth for tooth and mass destruction weapon for mass destruction weapon. Nagai's story, however, is based upon pessimism that there is no justice in war, any war, and it doesn't bring a bright future. It is contradictory to Goethe who justifies the union with the devil Mephistopheles for a personal ambition and prosperity following the extremely optimistic philosophical assumptions of the Enlightenment.

The philosophy of the Enlightenment with the emphasis on man's might and intelligence, popular and fashionable from the mid 18th century and 19th century in Europe, totally bankrupted and collapsed to the ground. In the 19th century in the era of the Meiji restoration (1868), a bourgeois revolution took place in Japan. The leaders of the new government were inspired by the Enlightenment philosophy in the West and created a modern military state based on the hybridization of traditional Japanese and Western philosophies and new technologies. It failed, however, in Japan's defeat in the Second World War. Nagai was born in the age of Japan's defeat and so did not directly witness the end of the military state and the Japanese version of the Enlightenment. He did, however, grow up in the atmosphere of anti-war sentiment, aversion against mass destruction weapons and pessimism on militarism.

Devil Lady

In 1997, Go Nagai revamped the series and created Devilman Lady (Devil Lady in the U. S.). Devil Lady is based on Go Nagai's idea of "What if the main character was a woman?" The story takes a different approach to what is presented in its Devilman counterpart. In Devil Lady, a woman named Jun Fudo learns that she has the power to transform into a being known as a "devilman" or "Devil Beast". A woman named Ran Asuka shows up and explains to her that her "powers" or "gifts" are actually believed to be somewhat of a disease known as the "Devil Beast Syndrome". It is even stated that these "devilmen" are actually the next step in human evolution as a means of survival. The story became very popular and was made into an anime series in 1998. The series consists of 26 episodes and was released in the U. S. during late 2002 and early 2003. The Devil Lady series is very popular and contains its own original story that stands out from the Devilman series.

Devil Lady (デビルマンレディー "Debiruman Redī," or "Devilman Lady") Jun Fudo lives in a city terrorized with beast-like humans and is secretly recruited to rid the city of them.

Story (Original Manga)

The original manga was the Devil Lady which was created in1997, a year before the TV series started. The manga storyline is more violent and sexually oriented, like a pornographic comic. The manga shows a depiction of many of the characters being tortured, raped and other grotesque and controversial descriptions.

Jun Fudo was a teacher who raised her younger brother, Hikaru. One day, as she and a group of students go on an outdoor trip, Jun begins to experience unusual nightmares. Then a group of demons, martial artists in human form in a nearby chalet, attempt to rape Jun and the female students. As she was being violated, Jun felt her soul being ripped apart and because of this, a terrifying transformation occurs turning her into the Devil Lady. She protects the girls who have survived the demon attacks and kills the demons with her newfound strength. Suddenly, a woman named Lan Asuka or a female version of Ryo Asuka appears and says that she was the one who had awakened the sleeping beast within Jun.

Anime TV Series

The Devil Lady of the anime TV Series has storyline that is almost completely different from the manga, featuring only two characters from the original manga, Jun Fudo and Lan Asuka. Also, because it is being shown on television, the sex and violence that is given in the manga had to be toned down.

In the Anime version, Jun is a successful supermodel in Tokyo instead of a teacher. She is a very quiet and timid and prefers to avoid most social interactions, with two exceptions. She is generally open with her manager and outrightly friendly with an aspiring teen model named Kazumi. As the series progresses she becomes much more independent. She is the second human with devil beast syndrome capable of retaining her ability to reason.

Jun's alter ego, Devil Lady is the exact opposite of Jun. She is loud, violent, and temperamental. Her unforgiving and aggressive nature tends to make all of her battles very graphic. Her appearance is basically a female version of Devilman.

Lan Asuka is the woman who scouted Jun for the Human Alliance, and is a high-ranking government official. She is a cold, aggressive, and manipulative woman, who cares nothing for the people who work under her. When she forced Jun to confront the Devil-beast Wolver, she had no concern for Jun's survival, her theory that Jun was a Devil-beast was based only on a hunch. As the series progresses, even though she is cruel to Jun, she cares about Jun's safety. She acts as Jun's liaison and tells her when and where a beast will appear. She seems to have different intentions from her organization and does a great deal of work without their knowledge. Besides this, Lan Asuka is a female version of Lucifer although she inherited several attributes from Ryo Asuka.

Although Devil Lady is a female version of Devilman, there is no Faustian theme, anti-war, anti-Enlightenment or in-depth demonology in it. Jun Fudo neither possesses the tragic character nor a deep existential agony as Akira who chooses a union with Amon to gain a power over other dark angels, having abandoned his humanity. Unlike Akira, Jun has a union with a demon simply for convenience, therefore experiences little regret about it. It is understandable that Jun who belongs to a nearly two decades younger generation than Akira is more opportunistic than the older generation and does not feel agony, sorrow or regret for losing humanity.

Hellboy: American Inspiration of Devilman

Hellboy is a 2004 supernatural action-thriller film directed by Guillermo Del Toro. Hellboy, the protagonist of the story is a demon from an alternate dimension like Amon. Hellboy, possibly a product of an inspiration from Devilman, stands a couple feet taller than anyone, smokes a cigar and fights demons. Unlike Amon/Devilman, however, he doesn't grow into gigantic "Ultraman size" or shrink when he is in a fighting mode.

Story (Movie)

In 1944, the German Nazis work with Russian mystic *Grigori Rasputin* on an isolated island off the coast of Scotland to build a dimensional portal, integrating modern technology and paranormal science. Rasputin , who had been long dead, comes back to life from the Hades by the magic or occult practice several times.

Nazis intend to use the dimensional portal, with Rasputin's help, to awaken the Ogdru Jahad or the Seven Gods of Chaos, monstrous entities that had been imprisoned and asleep since an unspecified remote past, in order to destroy their enemies. They are locked up in a different demension and stayed dormant over a millennium in the same way demons in Devilman or Rita Repulsa and her followers in *Mighty Morphin Power Rangers* (1993). Rasputin secretly attempts to use the entities to bring about the destruction of the entire Earth. He is aided by his servant and lover, Ilsa von Haupstein, whom he has granted eternal life, and Nazi Colonel (Sturmbannführer) Karl Ruprecht Kroenen, a notorious assassin. The United States sends a small Army team to destroy the portal, guided by a young doctor, Professor Trevor Bruttenholm, who is well-versed in terms of sorcery and paranormal studies. In the ensuing battle, the German scientists and soldiers are killed and the portal is destroyed, killing Rasputin. Ilsa and Kroenen escape capture. As the Army team surveys the ruins for anything that may have sneaked into their dimension through the portal, they discover a bright red infant demon with a right hand seemingly made from stone. Bruttenholm coaxes it into his arms with a Baby Ruth candy bar. They name the little demon "Hellboy" and raised him with human children.

Sixty years later, a young FBI agent named John Myers is transferred to the Bureau of Paranormal Research & Defense, run by Professor Bruttenholm. He is introduced to Hellboy, now an adult. There is also an amphibian humanoid with a fish-like appearance named Abe Sapien who has advanced psychic abilities, and Liz Sherman, a pyrokinetic human female who has yet to learn to control her fire starting abilities. Liz has recently left the bureau (for the 13th time) and checked herself into a mental hospital in an effort to protect others from her talent. Despite regular visits and coaxing from Hellboy, who appears infatuated with her, she is determined not to return.

Meanwhile, Kroenen and Ilsa resurrect Rasputin. Rasputin and his companions travel to New York and the Machen Library of Paranormal Artifacts. There, they open a display and, through magic, release a demon known as Sammael, a hell-hound with a distinct Lovecraftian appearance. Rasputin imbues Sammael with the power to reincarnate and split his essence, causing two of the creatures' "eggs" to hatch and mature in seconds each time one dies. Rasputin then visits Liz as she sleeps, reactivates her powers and causes the near-total destruction of the hospital. Afterwards, Myers talks to her, and convinces her to return to the bureau, at least for the short term.

Liz's vital signs are gone when Hellboy returns from the fight with the army of Rasputin, but he whispers into her ear, and suddenly her life is restored. When she asks how her soul was returned, Hellboy replies that he told the creatures from the other side, "Hey, you on the other side. Let her go. Because for her I'll cross over, and then you'll be sorry." She and Hellboy kiss as she surrounds them in blue flame, and the narrator, Myers, says what truly makes a man is "Not how he starts things, but how he decides to end them."

Difference between Devilman & Hellboy

Hellboy, possibly a product of an inspiration from Devilman. has many similarities to the hero created by Go Nagai. Unlike Amon/Devilman, however, he doesn't grow into gigantic "Ultraman size" or shrink when he is in a fighting mode. At the same time, contrary to Amon who was already thousands of years old when he wakes from a long sleep and is discovered under ice, Hellboy was a mere infant when Professor Trevor Bruttenholm found him in a dimensional portal. Amon/Devilman, possibly one of original fallen angels who followed Lucifer, was already older than the history of the entire human race when the story begins. On the other hand, Hellboy is only 60 years old in the year 2004, and as a demon, he is extremely young.

Also, unlike Amon, he does not merge with a human and his personality is not affected by a human host. His is always Hellboy from his birth, has no human component unlike Devilman, although he grew up in human culture. Therefore, in the story of Hellboy, there is no Faustian theme or tragedy and heroism of a demonized man who acquired the power of a fallen angel for a larger good. Also unlike Nagai's masterpiece, the storyline of Hellboy does not seem to have an apocalyptic dynamism or end time theme. The current story ends with a peaceful and humorous scene, yet some future work may develop into an apocalyptic climax with the total destruction of humanity. And because Hellboy hasn't merged with a human, he has no human form to transform into when he is not in a battle mode. For the same reason he does not enjoy the same convenience and privacy as Devilman who is capable of living, as Akira Fudo, among humans when he is not fighting enemies.

The main antagonist of Hellboy is Rasputin, an immortal mystic or sorcerer who died and came back to life several times as opposed to Lucifer or any other demons. The historical Rasputin, a charismatic healer and mystic born in 1869 was well known for his peculiar teaching and bizarre practice and lifestyle. After he earned fame as a mystic teacher and "prophet," Rasputin befriended the Tsar and became an advisor in his court. The Tsar referred to Rasputin as "our friend" and a "holy man," a sign of the trust that the family placed in him. Rasputin had a considerable personal and political influence on the Imperial family, and the Tsar and the Empress considered him a man of God and a religious prophet. However, he exhibited several bizarre conducts in the court and disgusted many. For example, he exposed his genitals during a dinner and washed them in a wine pitcher in front of both men and women, calling it a "holy rite." He died in 1916 and became a legendary person likely because of his eccentricity. After his death, many authors wrote stories about Rasputin and transformed him into an immortal demonic character. He came back to life in several novels or cinema stories including Disney's *Anastasia* (1997), an Academy Award nominated animated musical film. Although he was a trusted court advisor of the Tsar, posthumous Rasputin in Disney's Anastasia is a villain who curses the young princess in the underworld and persistently seeks her life. In the same way as the story of Anastasia, demonic posthumous Rasputin plays an important role as a major villain in Hellboy.

Although, the author of the Hellboy has a similar fascination with the demonic world as Nagai, there is no agony and tragic theme of a man who dares to choose a union with a demon to gain a power over the troops of dark angels, having abandoned his humanity. Contrary to the Devilman story with its apocalyptic conclusion with a final war that wipes out all of humanity, the Hellboy film ends with a humorous mid-credits scene, in which a forgotten and frightened Manning is lost several levels down in the dank and dim halls of the mausoleum.

Go Nagai. All Illustrations: World of Devilman. Kodansha, Tokyo: Japan, 1998.[81]

---

[81] The picture is used under "fair dealing" (Canada) and "fair use" (USA) provisions in copyright law.

Part 2 - Mechanical deities in Mazinger Series and Greco Roman mythology

Nagai is also known as the creator of Mazinger series who developed the concept of giant robots that are able to transform. He created the Mazinger Z, later expanded to Great Mazinger, God Mazinger and Mazinkaiser in which he developed the concept of giant mecha. This idea became strongly productive in many television programs in Japan. Mazinger is, in fact, considered the first successful "Super Robot" anime show, and has spanned numerous imitations that continue today. The Mazinger series clearly exhibitsNagai's fascination with the ancient Greco-Roman world to the readers and viewers in the same way as the Devilman series show his strong interest in the Biblical narratives. Mazingers were not only giant mecha, but robotic deities and the storylines and characters were based on Greek mythology.

Mazinger Z

Mazinger Z (マジンガーZ Majingā Zetto), known as Tranzor Z in North America, is a manga series by Go Nagai, serialized in Shueisha Shonen Jump from October 1972. In December of the same year, an anime adaptation premiered on Fuji Television. The TV series ended September 1, 1974, outliving its manga counterpart. The storyline features Professor Juzo Kabuto was a brilliant scientist who constructs the super-robot Mazinger Z. Since this machine would have power rivaling even a god or devil, Kabuto named it Mazinger Z (from the Japanese words "Ma" (魔), demon, and "Jin" (神), god).

Story

Mazinger Z is a gigantic Super Robot, constructed with a fictitious metal called Super-Alloy Z (Chogokin Z), which is forged from a new element mined from a reservoir found only in the sediment of Japan's Mt. Fuji. The mecha was built by Professor Juzo Kabuto as a secret weapon against the forces of evil, represented in the series by the Mechanical Beasts of Dr. Hell, the main evildoer of this series. Dr. Hell is a German member of a Japanese archeological team who discovers ruins of a lost pre-Grecian civilization on an island named Bardos; the civilization was loosely based on the ancient Mycenae, and was called the Mycene Empire in the series. One of their findings was that the Mycene used an army of steel titans about 20 m in height like Titans in the Greek myth. Finding prototypes of those titans underground that could be remote-controlled and realizing their immense power on the battlefield, Dr. Hell becomes insane and has all the other scientists of his research team killed except for Professor Kabuto. The lone survivor manages to escape back to Japan and attempts to warn the world of its imminent danger. Meanwhile, Dr. Hell establishes his headquarters on a mobile island and plans to use the Mechanical Beasts in order to become the new ruler of the world. To counter this, Kabuto constructs Mazinger Z, a formidable super-robot made of Super-Alloy Z and manages to finish it just before being killed by a bomb planted by Hell's right-hand man, Baron Ashura. Ashura is a half-male, half-female creature whose name is stems from Asura, a Hindu deity of war, rather than a Greek god.[82] Ashura is one of Dr. Hell's numerous creations made of a men and woman long dead. [83] As Dr. Kabuto is dying, he manages to inform his grandson Kouji Kabuto about the robot and its use. Kouji becomes the robot's pilot, and in every episode afterwards

---

82 Wikepedia: Asura. Was available March 2009: http://en.wikipedia.org/wiki/Asura

83 Baron Ashura was originally two separate individuals. Long ago, a man and woman fell in love, but their love was forbidden and upon discovery, they were mummified and buried alive. Many years later, a huge chunk of rubble landed between the two corpses, destroying the man's right half and the woman's left half. Eventually, Dr. Hell stumbled upon the tomb and discovered them. Somehow, he sewed the two remaining halves together and then brought the composite being to life. Dubbing his creation Baron Ashura, Dr. Hell used him/her as his main henchman. In response, Baron Ashura swore loyalty to Dr. Hell.

battles both the continuous mechanical monsters and the sinister henchmen sent by Doctor Hell.

Learning to pilot the giant machine, Kouji swears to defend the Earth in his grandfather's place. Though Mazinger Z would serve Kouji to battle the Mechanical Monsters, he finds himself outclassed by the stronger battle beasts unleashed by the Mycene Empire. Mazinger Z is badly damaged until it is rescued by the Great Mazinger and its pilot, Tetsuya Tsurugi. Kouji and Mazinger Z belong to the Photon Power Lab headed by Dr. Yumi, a close colleague of Dr. Kabuto. Sayaka Yumi daughter of Professor Yumi is also selected as a pilot of a female robot robot Aphrodite A and later Venus A to assist Kouji. [84]

Great Mazinger

Great Mazinger (グレートマジンガー Gurēto Majingā) is the name of a manga comic book and anime television series by manga artist Go Nagai, made as a direct continuation of the successful Mazinger Z series. It was aired in Japan in 1974 immediately following the end of the first Mazinger series. It lasted for 56 episodes.

Story

The story centers on Tetsuya Tsurugi, an orphan raised by Dr. Kenzo Kabuto, the once thought dead father of Mazinger Z pilot Koji Kabuto and son of Dr. Juzo Kabuto who created Mazinger Z. Kenzo Kabuto is the creator of the new, improved version of Mazinger, made by refining his father's Super Alloy Z (Chogokin Z) into a new, stronger form named Super Alloy New Z (Chogokin New Z), designed to fight against humanity's new enemy, the Mikenese Empire, led by the Great General of Darkness and his army of robots. Kenzo gives the Great

---

84 Mazinger Z (Wiki) http://en.wikipedia.org/wiki/Mazinger_Z

Mazinger to Tetsuya to pilot, who is accompanied by a new token girl, June Hono, half Japanese, half African-American girl who was also an orphan, in her female robot Venus A.

With the original Mazinger Z destroyed, Kouji travels to America to study space travel and leaves Japan's defense in the hands of Tetsuya and the Fortress of Science of which his father Kenzo was the head. Both Great Mazinger's and Tetsuya's training are completed just in time to come to Kouji's aid as the Mycene Battle Beasts overwhelm Mazinger Z. Mycene Battle Beasts are titanic cyborgs who posess the same body as Dr. Hell's Mechanical Monsters and live brains of ancient Mycenaean warriors. Tetsuya battles the Mycene Battle Beasts and their mighty generals, culminating in a bitter final battle with the Mycene's military leader, Great General of Darkness. Later, after the defeat and death of Great General of Darkness, the Mycene Empire revives Dr. Hell as Great Marshall of Hell to replace the late general. Mycene the Empire begins a last-ditch assault while the Great Mazinger and Tetsuya are recovering from their final fight with Great General of Darkness with a formidable cyborg body the same size as Great Mazinger.

Both Great Mazinger's and Tetsuya's training are completed just in time to come to Kouji's aid as the Mycene Battle Beasts overwhelm Mazinger Z. Both Kouji and the Mazinger Z return, stronger than before, in order to save the Photon Power Plant. But they fail to save the Science Fortress and his father Kenzo. Together with the returned Great Mazinger, Boss Borot, Diana A and Venus A, the Mycene are destroyed.

The series also includes some cast members from the original Mazinger Z show, such as Shiro Kabuto (Koji's little brother) and comic-relief character Boss and his robot Boss Borot.

Mazinkaiser

Mazinkaiser (マジンカイザー Majinkaizā) is an anime OVA series and altered story of Mazinger Z and Great Mazinger together, inspired by Go Nagai's Mazinger series. The OVA follows Kouji Kabuto, Tetsuya Tsurugi and the rest of the "Mazinger Team" as they fight against Dr. Hell's Mechanical Beasts. In one of their epic battles, the Mazinger Team suffers a crushing defeat at the hands of Dr. Hell and his minions after Mazinger Z is stolen and its pilot, the legendary Kouji Kabuto, is rendered missing in action. When Dr. Hell's second-in-command Baron Ashura uses Mazinger Z, Kouji makes a surprise return in Mazinkaiser - an all-new Mazinger with heavier armor and deadlier attacks.

Story

An army of machines, led by Baron Ashura, defeats Kouji's Mazinger Z and Tetsuya's Great Mazinger. In the aftermath, Kouji stumbles upon a forgotten laboratory. Inside he finds Mazinkaiser, the most powerful robot ever built. The series chronicles Kouji's experience with the machine as he copes with Kaiser's power while defeating Dr. Hell's forces.

This Episode introduces the Mazinkaiser version of Venus A, piloted by Sayaka instead of June Hono from Great Mazinger series. Toward the end of the series, Dr. Hell launches a full scale assault on the Photon Power Lab, using a Mechanical Beast to infect Venus A and turn it against them. Then, Nagai uncovers an upgraded version of Great Mazinger to save Mazinkaiser and Venus A from the crisis. This Great is far more powerful than the one Tetsuya piloted in the previous episodes and is described as Shin Great Mazinger (the true Great Mazinger). The original Great Mazinger was the prototype version made by Dr. Kenzo Kabuto. At that time, Dr. Juzo Kabuto, thought to be dead, was secretly making the final version of Great Mazinger in his underground laboratory.

God Mazinger

God Mazinger (ゴッドマジンガー Goddo Majingā) is another short-lived Mazinger anime series by Go Nagai. It is loosely based on his Mazinger Z, however, the story setting and characters have no connection with other Mazinger series. It aired on Japanese TV in 1983 and lasted for 23 episodes. Unlike other Mazinger series, the story setting of God Mazinger is an ancient Shamanic world of Mu the lost continent. Another characteristic that differentiates this story from other Mazingers is a strong inclination to the historical fantasy genre rather than a mere science fiction anime. The setting of God Mazinger was the amalgamation of Nagai's unique and dynamic micro-cosmos in which gigantic mecha, futuristic weapons or vehicles from the science fiction and swords and armors from the antiquity to the mediaeval world. It is also significant that the lost civilization Mu in God Mazinger is ruled by a shaman queen Aira who resembles Himiko, an ancient Japanese queen.

Story

The protagonist and the pilot of God Mazinger is Japanese teen Yamato Hibino who travels into the past through a time warp. Yamato, a high school student in the late 20th century is called by a "majin" or divine entity named God Mazinger in the lost continent Mu that sunk into the ocean 10,000 years ago. The dinosaur army of the Dragonia Empire threatens the world, and Queen Aira of Mu needs Yamato to help her fight back with the aid of the stone-made "majin" or a divine entity God Mazinger, the guardian of the entire civilization that looks like a giant robot. Upon his arrival, people of Mu Empire praise Yamato as a true hero or even "Messiah" like figure. Their opponent is Emperor Dorado and his son Prince Eldo, whose vendetta against Yamato was just beginning when the show was canceled. The series is considered as part of the Mazinger saga, if not only for the name of the title and that of his creator.

UFO Robo Grendizer

UFO Robo Grendizer (UFOロボ・グレンダイザー, UFO Robo Gurendaizā), is another super robot show created by manga artist Go Nagai and a Mazinger spinoff, since the storyline has a link with Mazinger series except God Mazinger. It was shown on Japanese TV in 1975 and lasted 74 episodes. Grendizer was also part of Jim Terry's Force Five series under the title Grandizer. Grendizer is a giant robot that interfaces with Spazer, a flying saucer that enables the robot to fly.

Unlike Kouji and Tetsuya in the Mazinger series, the protagonist is the extraterrestrial Prince of Planet Fleed, who piloted under the guise of the masked warrior Duke Fleed. Like Mazinger Z and Great Mazinger, it was popular in European and Arab countries, especially France and Egypt. The name Duke Fleed could be taken from Siegfried a hero and dragon slayer in various myths and legends in Europe. The series were popular in these countries likely due to the fact that the legend of Duke Fleed is permeated through the memory of populations in Europe and Middle East as a part of the collective unconscious.

Story

The homeworld of the Vega Empire is becoming unstable due to the exploiting of Vegatron, a powerful radioactive substance. Seeking to expand his militaristic empire and to find a substitute planet on which to settle, the ruthless King Vega unleashes his armies — composed of flying saucers and giant robotic monsters — and turns first against neighbors such as the Planet Fleed, a highly advanced but peaceful world. In an ironic twist, the invaders' blitzkrieg turns against them. The once verdant, idyllic Fleed is turned into a radioactive wasteland. But the only known survivor of the royal family, Prince Duke Fleed, steals the Grendizer, the robotic embodiment of the Fleedian God of War from the Vegan invaders who plan to use it to spearhead their invasion fleet.

Fleeing Vegan space by flying at faster than light speed, Duke enters the solar system and switches course to Earth, landing on the slopes of Mount Fuji. He is befriended by Dr. Umon, a noted scientist who oversees a research laboratory near a small ranch. The kindly Umon takes in the young alien as his son, under the assumed name of Daisuke, and assists him in hiding Grendizer. Taking the name Daisuke Umon, Duke Fleed works at the ranch run by Danbei Makiba.

Approximately two years later, Kouji Kabuto returns to Japan after studying abroad in a flying saucer he personally designed and built (called the TFO). He heads to the laboratory after hearing of multiple sightings of "flying saucers". He plans to contact the aliens and make peace with them. Daisuke, however, fears that the alien Vegans, led by generals Blaki and Gandal, are preparing to attack Earth. Kouji ignores the warnings and flies out to meet the incoming saucers. In order to save Kouji and protect his adoptive homeworld from destruction, Daisuke is forced to return to his true identity as Duke Fleed. He unearths Grendizer from its hiding place under the lab and sets off to fight his enemies.

The Vegans establish a base on the dark side of the moon and start to attack Earth from there. Kouji discovers Duke Fleed's true identity and their bitter rivalry soon turns to friendship. The daughter of Danbei Makiba, Hikaru, also discovers Daisuke's secret and becomes a pilot in order to assist him despite his objections. Later on, it is revealed that there were two more survivors from planet Fleed: Duke's younger sister Maria Grace Fleed and a man who had rescued her and fled to Earth, raising her under the guise of her grandfather.

King Vega gathers his remaining forces and makes an all-out attack on Earth, destroying the Moon Base to coax his troops into fighting to the end and finally succeeds in invading Earth and taking it as their new home planet. Duke and company go out to intercept them in Grendizer and the newly-designed space combat Spazers. Near the end of the series, it also revealed that Duke Fleed was once engaged to King Vega's daughter, Princess Rubina, prior to the Vegan invasion to Fleed. When Rubina discovers that planet Freed was no longer polluted with Vegatron radiation and that her fiancé was alive on the distant planet Earth, she rushes to bring him the good news. One of Vega's generals ambushes Duke Fleed, and Rubina is killed when she shoots at Duke. After a fierce battle, they destroy the Vegan mothership along with King Vega. Then Duke and Maria return to help reconstruct planet Fleed.

Gigantic Robots & Mythology

The Mazinger series was not shown in the United States for more than a decade after its creation. It was, however, shown unedited and in its entirety in Greece, Italy, Mexico and other Latin American countries with great success. This is possibly because Great Mazinger's story has a strong link with Greco-Roman mythology and Mediterranean culture such as the Mycene Empire, so that viewers from the Latin cultures can feel familiar with the storyline and underlying theme. On the other hand, North American viewers, with less knowledge about Greco-Roman history, did not grasp the background of the story in the same way as the Greek and Latin population. So that they failed to enjoy the story with Japanese made giant robot battles against the ancient Mycene Empire.

In all stories of the Mazinger series we can easily see Nagai's fascination with the ancient civilizations and deities. All characters and mecha in the Mazinger narratives were taken from the mythological world and followed the theme of either Greek or Japanese heroic stories. But God Mazinger has a stronger inclination to reflect Nagai's mythologicalism.

Mycenae (Greek Μυκ ναι), is an archaeological site in Greece, located about 90 km south-west of Athens, in the north-eastern Peloponnese. Argos is 6 km to the south; Corinth, 48 km to the north. From the hill on which the palace was located one can see across the Argolid to the Saronic Gulf. In the second millennium BC Mycenae was one of the major centres of Greek civilization, a military stronghold that dominated much of southern Greece. The period of Greek history from approximately 1600 BC to approximately 1100 BC is called Mycenaean.

Much of the Mycenean religion survived into classical Greece in their pantheon of Greek deities, but it is not known to what extent Greek religious belief is Mycenean. There are several reasonable guesses that can be made. Mycenean religion was almost certainly polytheistic, and the Myceneans were actively syncretistic, adding foreign deities to their pantheon of deities with regularity. At some point in their cultural history, the Myceneans adopted the Minoan goddesses and associated these goddesses with their sky-deities. Interestingly enough, in Nagai's Mazinger series, all Mycenean robots and titanic cyborgs that are as long as Mazingers, fly like the sky-god.

Several characters like half-man and half-tiger Archduke Gorgon, a titanic cyborg Minister Argos and Superhuman General Julicaesar seem to have stemmed from Greco-Roman world. A few other Myceneans Titans with Greek names are

Akilleus, Iscarius, Hercules, Barbaras and Helena. Among them, Helena is a tragic character who has forgotten her identity as a Warrior Beast because of living as a human for too long. She refuses to fight against Great Mazinger and the humanity following the order of her superiors in the Mycenae Empire. Eventually, when a microchip inside of her body activates her true identity as a mechanical beast, she fights Great Mazinger and is destroyed in battle. In a sense, she is as tragic as Helen of Troy in Greek mythology because she has no choice over her destiny. Nagai also named female robots Aphrodite A, Venus A, and Diana A after Greek goddesses.

God Mazinger & Shamanism

Mecha in God Mazinger were not simply machines, but deities and spiritual beings more literally than those in other Mazinger narratives. Unlike other Mazingers, God Mazinger owns his own soul and personality besides the one which belongs to the pilot. When Yamato the pilot boards the Mazinger, his personality and Mazinger's own soul are merged into one consciousness. And the theme of Mazinger as a bio-mechanical entity with its own soul instead of simply a machine is passed into later productions like North American *The Transformers: The Movie* (1986) and Hideaki Anno's Neon Genesis Evangelion (1995) that I will be introduced in the next chapter.

Besides that, God Mazinger had the story setting of the lost civilization Mu and followed the theme of Shamanism, while all other three Mazingers (Mazinger, Mazinger Z and Mazinkaiser) followed Greek mythological themes. Mu is now considered by the majority of scholars to be a hypothetical and fictional continent that allegedly existed in one of Earth's oceans. In the past, however, authors like Augustus Le Plongeon (1825–1908) and James Churchward (1851–1936) claimed that Mu actually existed like Maya and Atlantis in a remote past.[85]

[85] Wikepedia: Mu (lost continent). Was available March 2009: http://en.wikipedia.org/wiki/Mu_(lost_continent)

Churchward claimed that Mu was the common origin of the great civilizations of Egypt, Greece, Central America, India, Burma and others, including Easter Island, and was in particular the source of ancient megalithic architecture.[86] In a shamanic society the magic and rites of mysticism ruled day to day activities and the chief shaman/shameness or priest/priestess who had access to the spiritual world and performed these mystical rites was usually the ruler of the society.

In Nagai's understanding, Mu civilization had more similarity to the ancient Japan rather than Greece, being ruled by Shamanism like Proto-Shinto in Japan. In Nagai's God Mazinger, Mu is a shamanic society ruled by a shaman queen Aira who performs magic and mysticism like many other pre-historic or pre-literal civilizations in the antiquity.

According to historians, pre-literal Japan before the writing system was introduced from China, was also ruled by an obscure shaman queen named Himiko around the second century.[87] Like Himiko, Aira in Nagai's narrative is a unique combination of a queen and the priestess who serves the God Mazinger the deity who protects the empire. Also, the protagonist was named Yamato Hibino, a link with Prince Yamato Takeru,[88] a legendary hero from Kojiki or Japan's foundational myth. Although his real existence in history is questionable, Yamato Takeru is often the center of Japanese popular culture. Japanese authors and movie directors have produced numerous imaginative stories, live action or fantasy Sci-Fi movies loosely based on this prince.

Churchward also pointed to symbols from throughout the world, in which he saw common themes of birds, the relation

---

86 Lost Continent of Mu, the Motherland of Man (1926)
87 Wikepedia: Himiko (queen). Was available May 2009: http://en.wikipedia.org/wiki/Himiko_(queen)
88 Wikepedia: Yamato Takeru. Was available May 2009: http://en.wikipedia.org/wiki/Yamato_Takeru

of the Earth and the sky, and especially the Sun. He claims the king of Mu was Ra and he relates this to the Egyptian god of the sun, Ra, and the Rapanui word for Sun, ra'a, which he incorrectly spells "raa". He claimed to have found symbols of the Sun in "Egypt, Babylonia, Peru and all ancient lands and countries...a universal symbol". In fact, the also have the Sun as a symbol in their flag, and they have worshipped the Sun goddess Amaterasu from the pre-literal era. Therefore, it is easy to speculate that Nagai created the image of the lost civilization Mu based on his knowledge of pre-historic, pre-literal Japan ruled by the Shaman Queen Himiko during the Shamanic era.

Grendizer & Siegfried the Dragon Slayer

The name Duke Fleed could be taken from Siegfried or Sigurd, a legendary hero and super-human dragon slayer in various myths, legends and modern theatre plays in Europe including a famous Ring of the Nibelungs (1876) by Richard Wagner (1813-1883). The story setting of UFO Robo Grendizer has an appearance of the fantasy world in the European legends transferred into space. In the Norse legend, Siegfried proves the legendary sword "Gram" has magical power to slay monsters. He agrees to kill Fafnir, who has turned himself into a dragon in order to be better able to guard the "gold".

Siegfried has Regin the blacksmith and his mentor make him a sword which he tests by striking the anvil, but the sword shatters. He has Regin make another one, but this also shatters. Finally, Siegfried has Regin make a sword out of the fragments that had been left to him by Sigmund his father. The resulting sword, Gram, cuts through the anvil proving to be good enough to kill Fafnir the evil dragon man.

Grendizer, the robotic embodiment of Fleedian God of War, parallels with Gram. The ruthless dictator King Vega and some of his followers could reflect the character of Fafnir. In the European mythological world in which Siegfried appears, "gold" is a symbol of multitude of meanings. However, the "gold" that Fafnir is obsessed with is the Rhine Gold which symbolizes power. The Rhine Gold is forged into a mighty ring named *Ring of the Nibelungs* which makes a person formidable and invincible. Later, the theme of the mighty gold ring is passed to J. R. R. Tolkien's (1892 – 1973) *Lord of the Rings* (1937). The rings in various stories are the source of power that almost every human being craves and the curse which makes ordinary human beings into monsters. In Nagai's Grendizer narrative, the Vega homeworld becomes unstable due to the exploiting of Vegatron, a powerful radioactive substance which could carry the same symbolism as the Rhine Gold. Vegatron is a curse which makes the entire race of Vegan formidable and their homeworld inhabitable.

Fafnir is so obsessed with power that he has loses his humanity and metamorphizes into a half-man and half-dragon monster. Likewise, King Vega is a monster obsessed with power. Nagai describes King Vega, the main villain of this series, as a grotesque monstrous character that somehow resembles a goblin in Teutonic myth or Ogre in European folklores, while at the same time his daughter, Princess Rubina is a beautiful blonde who closely resembles female humans. It might indicate that Vega might not be born with the same grotesque monstrous form but his deeds and actions are responsible for how he looks and what he is. On the other hand, Rubina who was once to marry the hero Duke Fleed retains her physical beauty because she does not abandon a gentle spirit although she is a part of the ruthless empire. Rubina has the same tragic fate as Brynhildr, a "shieldmaiden" and a valkyrie whom Siegfried meets after killing Fafnir. She pledges herself to him but also prophesies his doom and marriage to another. Likewise, the passionate love between Duke Fleed and Rubina ends up without fulfillment when one of the Vegan general strikes her starship.

All other main characters in the Vegan side like General Gandal, Colonel Blaki and Minister Zuril appear in grotesque monstrous forms that could indicate sharing the same obsession with the king they serve. Also, mechanical beasts of Vega empire are cyborgs like Mycene Battle Beasts with humanoid brains. They are brainwashed by the ideology of the empire and converted into Battle Beasts. Therefore, they have similarity to dragon men in the Norse legend who are obsessed with gold and lost humanity. The obsession of King Vega and all of his followers is summarized in one phrase, "Conquering the all milky way galaxy and then the entire universe".

At the end of the series, the entire empire of the dragons obsessed with "gold" in the space age is wiped out by the hero Duke Fleed, the Sci-fi anime version of Siegfried and his mighty Grendizer, the robotic embodiment of God of War.

Here, we can see Nagai's anti-war sentiment as in the Devilman in which Akira Fudo joins with the demon Amon, a Duke of Hell, and loses his humanity, to protect mankind from legions of demons. Likewise, many Vegan soldiers go through surgeries to join monstrous cyborg bodies and transforms into Vegan Battle Beasts to win in the battle. They made same kind of sacrifice to their nation and beloved monarchy as Japanese soldiers during the Second World War. The mighty Vegatron that may serve as the mass destruction weapon is the Sci-Fi version of the Rhine Gold that drives so many Vegan populations into madness and eventually extinction. Likely Nagai describes the Vegan Empire, the mighty formidable military state in space ruled by a ruthless dictator with an iron fist as a shadow of Imperial Japan prior to the Second World War.

Dynamic Mythological World of Go Nagai

[89] Go Nagai. Great Mazinger. onlyshonen.com, 2009.[90]

---

89 Was available August 2009: http://www.onlyshonen.com/mazingaznagai.htm
90 The picture is used under "fair dealing" (Canada) and "fair use" (USA) provisions in copyright law.

5

Apocalyptic Mecha Action: Neon Genesis Evangelion

(新世紀エヴァンゲリオン, Shin Seiki Evangerion)

Neon Genesis Evangelion, commonly referred to as NGE, Eva, or Evangelion, is a commercially and critically successful, influential and popular Japanese anime series that began in October 1995 and launched the Neon Genesis Evangelion franchise. It is commonly regarded as one of the greatest anime of all time. It was created by Gainax, written and directed by Hideaki Anno (b.1960), and co-produced by TV Tokyo and Nihon Ad Systems (NAS).

Evangelion is an apocalyptic mecha action series which centers around the efforts by the paramilitary organization *Nerv* to fight monstrous, biomechanical creatures called "Angels," primarily using giant mecha called Evangelions which are piloted by select teenagers, one of whom is the primary protagonist. The story follows these teenagers and other Nerv members moving to the final defeat of the Angels and the apocalyptic climax at the end.[91]

---

[91] Neon Genesis Evangelion (Wiki) http://en.wikipedia.org/wiki/Neon_Genesis_Evangelion

Events in the series refer to Judeo-Christian symbols from the book of Genesis and Biblical apocrypha among others. Later episodes shift the focus to psychoanalysis of the main characters who display various emotional problems and mental illnesses. The nature of existence and reality are questioned in a way that allows Evangelion to be characterized as "postmodern fantasy." Since Hideaki Anno, director of the anime series, had suffered from clinical depression prior to creating the series, one can speculate that the psychological aspects of the show are based on the director's own personal struggles with his illness.

Each pilot operates by synchronizing the pilot's soul[92] and the human soul inside the Eva via the enigmatic liquid substance known as LCL (Link Connect Liquid). It is used to mentally link a pilot with the Evangelion and supply oxygen directly to the lungs when breathed, similar to liquid breathing. LCL is a symbol of amniotic fluid which cushions and protects the fetus and helps the baby's lungs develop properly. Each Eva functions like mother's uterus and embraces the pilot like a baby. This maternal nature of Evangelions is one of the important themes of the entire story.

Along with the battles against the Angels, the central characters struggle to overcome their personal issues and personality conflicts that factor heavily into the events of the series and its eventual conclusion. Throughout the series, many of the main characters constantly have to cope with several social and emotional problems: characters are unwillingly forced to confront socially complex and challenging situations; unresolved sexual tensions grow between numerous characters; injuries, deaths, and defeats cause blows to their psyches; and previously steady relationships begin to falter.

---

92 In the context of Evangelion, a "soul" refers to an individual's conscious existence, mental structure and identity, rather than simply a conventional "supernatural" entity.

Plot (TV Series)

The basic storyline of Evangelion (Evas) begins with the invasion of Earth by gigantic, mysterious aliens with the mixed appearance of robotic and organic life forms called "angels." The beginning of the story is the year 2000 with the "Second Impact", a global cataclysm that almost completely destroys ice in Antarctica and leads to the deaths of half the human population of Earth. This plot could have been developed based on the rumors and popular stories about the "Y2K catastrophe" that spread around the world during the late 1990s. The "Second Impact" is believed by the public at large and even most of the *Nerv* organization to have been the impact of a mere meteorite landing in Antarctica, causing devastating tsunamis and a change in the Earth's axial tilt. This leads to devastating global climate change and subsequent geopolitical unrest, nuclear war and subsequent general economic distress. But the entire earth's population came to realize the presence of these "angels," caused the global catastrophe.[93]

The angels are strange creatures, seemingly bent on destroying the human species. They can only be defeated by the Evangelions, or giant bio-mechanical robots piloted by humans. The organization named Gehirn developed Evangelions in secret by cloning Angels. Gehirn is located inside the underground Geofront, which exists right underneath *Tokyo-3*, a militarized civilian city located on one of the last dry sections of Japan. Later, Nerv scientists discovered that the angels possessed similar DNA to humans.

Evas are similar creatures as angels with both robotic and organic attributes. These robots, however, can only be piloted by a select group of fourteen-year old children — including

---

[93] Neon Genesis Evangelion (anime) http://en.wikipedia.org/wiki/Neon_Genesis_Evangelion_(anime)

the main protagonist of the series, Shinji Ikari. This was because Evas are the bio-cybernetic entities which function as the extension of human bodies instead of simply machines. Therefore, the compatibility between each Eva and the pilot's genetic and psychological makeup is critical in the same way as artificial or donated live organs are to the recipient's body. At the same time, Shinji Ikari's father, Gendo Ikari, turns out to be the scientist responsible for the construction of the Evangelions.

Later, they also discoverthat the Second Impact is the result of contact with and experimentation on Adam: the first of the creatures that humans collectively named the Angels. The experiments were sponsored by the mysterious organization *Seele*, and carried out by the research organization *Gehirn*.

In the year 2010, Gehirn had accomplished a number of its scientific and engineering goals and corporately changed into the paramilitary organization Nerv. Nerv's central mission and objective is to locate and destroy the remaining Angels predicted by *Seele*. Nerv, however, has its own secret agenda. Gendo has *the Human Instrumentality Project*, that is the task of uniting all human minds into one global spiritual entity. Associated with Nerv is an institute that tasked with selecting and recruiting pilots for the Evangelions among the most capable children that are biologically compatible with Eva's organism.

Conventional weapons prove ineffective against the angels, largely due to its projected force field. Nerv takes command of the battles and is able to intercept and defeat the Angels using the Evangelions.

Not knowing why his father summoned him, Shinji Ikari, a 14 year old boy who chronically suffers from anxiety, depression, lack of self confidence and loneliness, arrives to Tokyo-3 just as the Third Angel attacks the city. Shinji reluctantly agrees to join Nerv to pilot *Evangelion Unit 01*, and begins living with Captain (later Major) Misato Katsuragi. He and Rei Ayanami battle the successive advances of the Angels together and are later joined by Asuka Langley Soryu, the pilot of Unit 02. Surrounded by LCL (Link Connect Liquid), the pilot's nervous system, mind and body join with the Eva's controls, allowing the Eva to be controlled by the pilot's thoughts and actions. The higher a pilot's synchronization ratio, the better the pilot can control the Eva, and therefore fight the enemy more effectively. The drawback of LCL control is that the pilot experiences physical and mental pain proportionate to that experienced by the Eva. At a high enough synch ratio, injuries to the Eva may even be mimicked within the body of the pilot, potentially leading to severe injury and/or death. Almost all of the pilots are hospitalized multiple times throughout the series.

While Ritsuko mentions at the series' beginning that the Evas do have some biological components to them, the extent to which the Evas are biological is not immediately apparent. Unit 01 is connected to Yui Ikari, Gendo's wife, since it absorbed her body and soul in a failed experiment. This could indicate that Evangelion also carries the motif of *Oedipus Rex* written by Sophocles (496 BCE - 406 BCE), since Shinji has a symbiotic union with Unit 01 who possesses his mother's soul, while having a serious conflict with his father. Rei herself is suspected to be a partial clone of Yui, and is known to harbor the soul of Lilith, the second Angel.

It is finally revealed, towards the end of the series, that the Evas are not "robots" or mere machines but are actually cloned Angels (Units 00, 02, 03, and 04 are made from Adam, and 01 is made from Lilith) into which mechanical components are incorporated as a means of restraint and control. This control is not perfect, as various units are shown over the course of the series driving into "berserk" mode, in which they can act of their own will, independent of any artificial power input.

In the end it is discovered that *the Human Instrumentality Project*'s true purpose is to force the completion of human evolution, and thereby save it from destroying itself. The plan is to break down the AT fields that separate individual humans, and in doing so, reduce all humans to LCL, or "primordial soup," the fundamental composite of human beings. All LCL would then be united into a supreme being, the next stage of humanity, ending all conflict, loneliness and pain brought about by individual existence. At the end of the series, Seele and Nerv come into direct conflict over the implementation of instrumentality.

In the last two episodes (the second set in 2016), Gendo and Rei initiate the Human Instrumentality Project, forcing several characters (especially Shinji) to face their doubts and fears and examine their self-worth. This ending was made up of flashbacks, strange, sketchy artwork, and flashing text "over a montage of bleak visuals, and a brief interlude depicting an "alternate" Evangelion universe. This alternative reality is not like the apocalyptic mecha genre. In fact, this enigmatic alternative universe seems to be a symbolism and representation of the psychic world and the path of internal and spiritual pilgrimage of Shinji and his colleagues. This is explored in greater depth in *Girlfriend of Steel*, eventually leading Shinji to conclude that life could be worth living and that he did not need to pilot an Eva to justify his existence, so he returns to his original reality.

The ambiguous and unclear meaning of this ending left many fans confused and unsatisfied and the author's intentionality remains in mystery. The final two episodes are possibly the most controversial segments of the Evangelion series and are received as flawed and incomplete by many. Anno and deputy director Kazuya Tsurumaki, however, defended the artistic integrity of the finale. From a post-modernist viewpoint, this ending would be considered well done and sends a message to the world that retains its artistic and philosophical integrity. Shinji finally discovered the true meaning of life and ultimate freedom at the end after successfully fighting his existential anguish.

The alternative reality that Shinji experienced through *the Human Instrumentality Project*, has some similarities to the world that Chihiro Ogino is slipping into in Hayao Miyazaki's *Spirited Away* (2003) as it contains an allegory and theme on the internal growth or the progression from childhood to maturity. The strange realities that take place in both Shinji's and Chihiro's life symbolize the internal battles that every human individual must endure.

The End of Evangelion (Film)

The End of Evangelion (新世紀エヴァンゲリオン劇場版 Shin seiki Evangerion Gekijō-ban: The End of Evangelion), a 1997 anime film written and directed by Hideaki Anno, won the Japan Academy Prize for popularity. The movie also won the Animage Anime Grand Prix prize for 1997. The film serves as the conclusion to the entire series. It begins shortly after the end of episode 24. Seele has realized Gendo's treachery and commands the JSSDF's forces to launch an all-out attack on Nerv headquarters. During the battle, Asuka Langley Soryu an Eva pilot realizes that she has a bond with Unit 02 and is not just its master and this bond gives her strength to battle the "mass-production" Evas, but she is ultimately defeated. Commander Misato Katsuragi who takes Shinji into Nerv headquarter battles her way past Seele's soldiers to get Shinji to his Eva but is mortally wounded. It is significant that the film depicts the apocalyptic completion of the Human Instrumentality Project, where individual identity is destroyed to create a single existence for all human beings - that is, people's AT-Fields are destroyed and the entirety of humanity is turned into LCL.

While Nerv is collapsing, Gendo attempts to implement Instrumentality by merging the embryonic Adam (bonded to his right hand) with Rei Ayanami, another Eva pilot. Rei, however, takes over the process and reunites with Lilith, who finally regains her soul, and creates an anti-AT Field. This causes the AT Fields of every human on Earth to break down, causing their bodies to dissolve into pools of LCL.

Instrumentality proceeds largely as planned; the souls of all human beings are absorbed into Lilith/Rei's body, causing her to grow into a supreme being of size comparable to the Earth. Rei gives control of the process to Shinji. His emotional suffering and loneliness prompts Shinji to accept this new form, believing that there could never be happiness in the real world. He goes through a series of mental journeys and monologue, eventually realizing that without pain there can be no joy, and to live with others is to experience joy as well as pain. This constitutes a rejection of the goal of Instrumentality – a world without the pain or joy of being a separate being.

At the end, the giant Lilith/Rei corrupts and falls apart, releasing the Anti-AT Field and allowing separate beings to come back into existence. Amidst the devastation, Asuka and Shinji are shown to have rematerialized from the sea of LCL, and in the last scene they find each other somewhere by the ruins of Tokyo-3. The giant Lilith/Rei who absorbed every human body and soul continues to grow until she finally falls apart resembling *No Face* (Kaonashi) in Miyazaki's Spirited Away (2001). No Face becomes intoxicated with the greedy atmosphere of the bathhouse and swells into a huge, aggressive monster, giving illusory gold to the bathhouse workers in exchange for lavish amounts of food. When the workers of Yubaba's bathhouse do not comply with his demands, he swallows several of them and grows larger and larger in the same way as Lilith/Rei. However, Sen/Chihiro or the protagonist feeds him an emetic, making him vomit up his tainted substance and the bath house workers and return to his original size. Both No Face and Lilith/Rei are leading the world to the catastrophic end as they gain enough power. But ultimately, both collapse and return into the original form before ending the world. It seems that both monsters are the products of negative human emotions like fear, greed, jealousy and hostility. They continue to grow until protagonists (Shinji and Chihiro) find solutions.

Both *Evangelion* and *Spirited Away* describe a series of mental journeys and personal and psycho-spiritual growth through the monologues or internal talks of the protagonists. Angels and monsters that Shinji and Chihiro grapple with in the two stories are strong representations of all we have to battle with in the same way as young David fights Goliath and defeats him (1 Samuel 17).

The meaning of *The End of Evangelion* is debated as to whether it is intended to enlarge and retell the TV episodes 25 and 26, the last portion of TV series. The film can be regarded as either an alternate ending to the TV version or as a more detailed, "real world" account of the ending found in the series' original ending in episodes 25 and 26, which takes place almost completely in the psyche of the main characters. *The End of Evangelion* episode reflects Shinji's point of view while inside the merged being or, alternatively, to completely replace the TV ending with a different one. Some believe that The End of Evangelion is an alternate ending to the series, perhaps created to please those fans who were displeased with the TV series' ending. Deputy Director Kazuya Tsurumaki said he felt the series was complete as it was.

However, there are several hints indicating that the movie portrays the physical aspects of the end of the series, while the last episodes of TV series deal with the interior, or emotional aspects, and the two form a whole. In TV episode 26', when *Instrumentality* is finally launched, Shinji questions himself about his life and what he really wishes. Shinji's lines and reflection process in this sequence are almost identical to what they were in TV episode 26, however in a much more condensed form. Similar reflections on the part of Asuka and Misato are also reflected (if briefly) in the film. Watching both thus allows a fuller understanding of the series. There were serious budget and schedule restraints in the later episodes of the series, and the film allowed for a more complete ending. During the TV series ending, a number of sketches from scenes that were later included in the movie are shown, hinting that the film, or something like the final production, was the intended finale all along. Indeed, the original script for episode 25 (which included, among others, a bloody fight between Asuka and the Eva Series) was abandoned due to censorship, budget and time restraints, yet the actual TV episode still featured some remnants of the first script (Misato and Ritsuko dead, Asuka inside her Eva in the water). Later, the original script was re-used for Episode 25: Air, a part of the End of Evangelion movie. Also, in the opening animation for the series, there are shots of Unit 01 with the angelic wings that it sprouts in Episode 26: *A Pure Heart For You*.

Characters

The characters of Evangelion are continuously struggling with their interpersonal relationships, the inner monsters or demons within, going through numerous traumatic events in their life that creates a complex pattern of interpersonal relationships. Throughout the story, these characters strive to establish their ego identities by going through various events as in the theory of psychosocial development articulated by Erik Erikson (1902 – 1994)[94].

---

94 Erik H. Erikson. Identity and Life Cycle. (New York, NY: The Norton &

Anno describes the hero, Shinji Ikari, as a boy who has completely withdrawn from human contact, and has "convinced himself that he is an insignificant and "unnecessary person,' so that he cannot even commit suicide." He describes Shinji and Misato Katsuragi as "extremely afraid of being hurt" and "unsuitable — lacking the positive attitude — for what people call heroes of an adventure." When compared to the stereotypical hero, Shinji is characterized more by lack of drives, energy, emotion and motivations than by any sort of heroism or bravery. In other words, he is a typical "anti-hero," a disqualified person as a hero in traditional story settings, but often replaces a hero in some unconventional narratives with a post-modern mindset. Rei Ayanami and Asuka Langley Soryu, the other major protagonists, have similar flaws and difficulty relating to others.

It is said that Anno, creating characters in Evangelion, made a bold attempt to make all perspectives into one in order to represent different aspects of life so that it might be impossible for everyone to arrive at a single theory. To some viewers, the characters are psychological representations in their own personal lives or even representations of viewers themselves, while to others, they are philosophical, religious, or historical symbols.

However the deeply pessimistic nature of the Evangelion series as well as the rarely seen huge array of problems in all the characters in it, draws viewers to a single question as to why there is no real happiness in the world presented in the story. Assistant Director Kazuya Tsurumaki said of the series, "But when all is said and done, Hideaki Anno's comments on 'Evangelion' + 'Evangelion' are that it is a message aimed at anime fans including himself, and of course, me too. If a person who can already live and communicate normally watches it, they won't learn anything."

Company, (1959/1980)

Inspiration & symbolism

Evangelion is dense with allusions to biological, military, religious and psychological concepts as well as numerous references or homages to older anime series (for example, the basic plot is seen in earlier anime like Space Battleship Yamato) – a tendency which inspired the nickname for the series, the "remixed anime." Anno's use of Freudian jargon and psychoanalytical theory as well as his allusions to religion and biology are often idiosyncratically used and redefined to carry his message. This tendency of Hideaki Anno has been criticized as "Total plagiarism!" and "just more mind games from the animation crew". Anno said:

"There is no longer room for absolute originality in the field of anime, especially given that our generation was brought up on mass-produced anime. All stories and techniques inevitably bring with them a sense of déjà vu. The only avenue of expression left open to us is to produce a collage-like effect based on a sampling of existing works."

"The people who make anime and the people who watch it always want the same things. The creators have been making the same story for about 10 years; the viewers seem to be satisfied and there's no sense of urgency. There's no future in that."

Regardless, Anno seems to have hoped to re-invigorate the genre of anime – seen as lifeless and moribund in the early 1990s – and restore originality, to create a new anime. This desire is also the reason Anno cited for creating the Rebuild of Evangelion movies: Many different desires are motivating us to create the new "Evangelion" film ... The desire to fight the continuing trend of stagnation in anime. The desire to support the strength of heart that exists in the world... Many times we wondered, "It's a title that's more than 10 years old.

Why now?" "Eva is too old", we felt. However, over the past 12 years, there has been no anime newer than Eva.

The interpretation of the symbols and concepts varies from individual to individual, and it is not clear how many are intentional or meaningful, or which are merely design elements or coincidences. Anno himself said, "It might be fun if someone with free time could research them." A number of these symbols were noted on the English DVD commentary for Death and Rebirth and End of Evangelion.

Many of the characters share their names with Japanese warships from the Second World War. such as the Sōryū, Akagi, and Katsuragi.. Other characters' names refer to other works of fiction, such as the two characters named after the protagonists of Ryu Murakami's (b. 1952) *Ai to Genso no Fascism* ("Fascism in Love and Fantasy"; the two main characters are named Aida Kensuke and Suzuhara Toji).

Psychology & Psychoanalytic Theories (Freud, Jung, Erikson & Frankl)

From the start, Evangelion invokes many psychological themes. Phrases used in episodes, their titles, and the names of the background music frequently derive from Sigmund Freud's works in addition to perhaps some Lacanian[95] influences in general Examples include "Thanatos", "Oral stage", "Separation Anxiety", and "Mother Is The First Other" (the mother as the first object of a child's love is the basis of the Oedipus complex). *Oedipus complex* is also one of many psychological themes in Evangelion series coming from Freudianism, since Shinji with a seriously conflicting relationship with his father, having a symbiotic union with Unit 01 who absorbed his mother's soul. The scenery and buildings in

---

95 Wikepedia: Jacques Lacan. Was available February 2009: http://en.wikipedia.org/wiki/Lacan

Tokyo-3 often seem laden with psychological import, even in the first episode.

The fourth episode has the English title Hedgehog's Dilemma, which is psychologically significant. The Hedgehog's Dilemma is a concept described by philosopher Arthur Schopenhauer (1788 – 1860) and later adopted by Freud. It describes a situation in which a group of hedgehogs all seek to become close to one another in order to share their heat during cold weather. Once accomplished, however, they cannot avoid hurting one another with their sharp quills. Though they all share the intention of a close reciprocal relationship, this may not occur for reasons which they cannot avoid. It is the subtitle of episode 4 and is mentioned in that episode by Misato Katsuragi as descriptive of her relationship with Shinji.

The theme of growth and maturity of the characters throughout the whole series could be explained in light of the developmental psychology articulated by Erik Erikson (1902 – 1994) and Freud. Evangelion's characters go through various life events striving to establish their ego identities almost following the theory of psychosocial development of Erikson's theory of human development. Throughout the story of Evangelion, there are themes of trust vs. mistrust; autonomy vs. shame and doubt; initiative vs. guilt; industry vs. inferiority; identity vs. role confusion; and finally intimacy vs. isolation.

The theme around LCL and the connection between Eva and the pilot seems parallel with Erikson's theme of trust vs. mistrust in the psychosocial crisis stage. These pilots act like fetus who are about to establish trusting relationships with their mothers in the amniotic sac, trying to synchronize with their Evas. Eva and the pilot within are connected with fluid called LCL in a mysterious way. Shinji could establish the synchronization or trusting relationship with his Eva Unit 01 one hand. On the other hand, Rei failed the synchronization with her Eva once and got almost killed.

Shinji's initial reluctance to pilot the Eva is well explained in light of the theme of autonomy vs. shame and doubt - the second Ericksonian theme of human development. Being the pilot of Eva Unit 01 was not linked to his autonomy. His lack of autonomy often frustrated Misato as well. In the episode 4, Shinji and Misato had a serious argument over his "attitude," and he left the Nerv organization. Shinji does his job because no one else is compatible with Eva Unit 01 and his father told him to do so. She told him that unless he really wants to do his job, he should never do it. Shinji doing his job without the sense of autonomy may symbolize typical second generation politicians, educators or business owners who do their jobs simply following their parents' expectations.

From the Eriksonian perspective, the Hedgehog's Dilemma is explained in light of the theme of *Intimacy vs. Isolation*. Though Shinji and Misato desired an intimacy or a close reciprocal relationship, they are reluctant to pursue it because they fear hurting each other like the hedgehogs. Through the intimacy we can reciprocate love and support and share the heat during cold weather. But the grim reality is that any close and intimate relationship has a risk factor of hurting each other. People who are afraid of intimacy tend to isolate themselves because they don't want to hurt themselves. Likewise, all other characters in Evangelion strive for intimacy yet are reluctant to pursue it and end up isolating themselves because they are not ready to pay the price of intimacy.

Many of the characters have deep psychological traumas in relation to their parents. Shinji's introversion and social anxiety stems from the death of his mother when he is young and his abandonment by his father. Asuka was the target of her mother's insanity, and discovered her mother's body after she hanged herself; her tough, bullying personality is a means of distracting herself from her pain, and she has made piloting Unit 02 her only source of pride and satisfaction. Misato's father neglected her when she was a child; after he was killed in the Second Impact, she stopped talking for a couple of years. In episode 25, Misato states that she was both attracted to and afraid of Ryoji Kaji because he reminded her of her father. Ritsuko saw her mother having an affair with Gendo Ikari; after her mother's suicide she felt both attraction and hate towards Gendo. Indeed, the last two episodes are "stripped of the high-tech gadgetry and the colorful visuals that characterize the earlier episodes in the series, these last two episodes take place largely in muted tones... a form of interrogation proceeds to be carried out as Shinji asks himself – or is asked by an unseen voice – probing psychological questions." The questions elicit unexpected answers, particularly the ones dealing with Shinji's motivation for piloting the Eva – he feels worthless and afraid of others (especially his father) if he is not piloting the Eva.

Asuka and Rei are also depicted in deep introspection and consideration of their psyches. Asuka comes to the realization that her entire being is caught up in being a competent Eva pilot and that without it, she has no personal identity: "I'm the junk... I'm worthless. Nobody needs a pilot who can't control her own Eva." Rei, who throughout the series has displayed minimal emotion, reveals that she has one impulse - Thanatos, an inclination to death: "I am Happy. Because I want to die, I want to despair, I want to return to nothing." In episode 25 Shinji and Asuka both show that they in fact suffered similar pasts but found different ways of dealing with it. This is further established in Shinji when he claims he has no life without Eva, but this is disproven by the world shown in Episode 26 followed by the famous "Congratulations" scene.

In summary, the connection between the Evas and their pilots, as well as the ultimate goal of the Human Instrumentality Project, bears a strong resemblance to Freud and Erikson's theories on internal conflict, interpersonal communication and psychosocial development. Also, angels and monsters that Eva pilots have to battle seem to be linked with certain archetypes in the psychic world, according to the Jungian theory. *Evangelion* characters go through a series of mental journeys and personal and psycho-spiritual growth through the monologues or internal talks of the protagonists in the same way as Miyazaki's *Spirited Away*. Both the angels and monsters seem to be stem from objects or archetypes from our collective unconscious domain.

This last episode also contains an existential theme. As Shinji experiences *Instrumentality*, he questions himself about the true meaning of life and what he really wishes. At the end of the last episode, Shinji finally discovers his own *raison d'être* and ultimate freedom that Viktor Frankl (1905 - 1997) discusses in his book Man's Search for Meaning (1946)[96]. Shinji fought the existential anguish successfully throughout the whole process of Instrumentality, which is followed by this "Congratulations" scene. This scene is similar to the one in Spirited Away (2003) that Chihiro received from her friends when she gave the correct answer to Yubaba asking, "Who are your parents among these pigs?" Both praises are like ones that students of Zen Buddhism receive from their masters when they obtain the right answers on their own and attain the state of "satori." Throughout the whole series, Evas conveys the same individuation narratives that O'Connor (1985) conceptualized in the same way as *Spirited Away* and promotes the audience to think about how we might reconcile our own individuation of the self. Throughout the whole series, there is a theme of individuation, or a psychological goal to reconcile internal opposites, such as our subconscious and conscious, or our shadow, irrational self with our objective, rational self in order to become whole.

---

96 Viktor E Frankl. Man's Search for Meaning. (Boston, MA: Beacon Press, 1946/2006).

Metaphors in Evangelion

Dennis Redmond (2007) contends that the Evas gradually evolved from a mere robotic appendage into a self-aware cybernetic organism with Godzilla-like body as the story progresses, and finally into powerful symbol of East Asian economic integration[97]. Evangelions are unique life-forms with both organic and robotic attributes like "zords" in *Mighty Morphin Power Rangers* (1993) or North American made Transformers (1986/ 2007). Redmond views the Evangelion as a symbol of post-modern and post-American era characterized by globalization and a borderless community. He points out that Anno looks down on both Americanism which once dominated the world and Japan's neo-nationalism with strong emphasis on the emperor centered value system and Shinto based worldview, as mere relics of the past. Redmond, therefore, understood the Japanese title "Shin Seiki (new century) Evangerion" as the new century in which both American domination and Japan's "keiretsu", or traditional nationalism based business community, has ended, and the English titled "Neon Genesis Evangelion" is the advent of a new era characterized by global corporations. Redmond stated that,

The transition to the post-American epoch is subtly encoded in the original Japanese title of the series, "Shinseiki Evangelion", which literally means, "Gospel of the New Century" (2007).

The Human Instrumentality Project (人類補完計画, Jinrui Hokan Keikaku, mankind complementation/completion plan) is the goal of the secret society Seele[98]. It is an attempt to artificially force the evolution of humanity, merging people's individual conscious minds into one single entity by dissolv-

---

97   Dennis Redmond. Anime and East Asian Culture: Neon Genesis Evangelion. Quarterly Review of Film and Video, 2007.

98   Wikepedia: Human Instrumentality Project. Was available September 2008: http://en.wikipedia.org/wiki/Human_Instrumentality_Project

ing the barriers (so-called AT Fields) between them, an event named the Third Impact. The *Human Instrumentality Project*, reducing all humans to LCL, which is revealed to be the "primordial soup," the fundamental composite of human beings. It is an attempt to join all human consciousness with a similar connection as Great Link of the shape-shifting species named Changelings in *StarTrek Deep Space Nine* (1993-1999. Changelings are life forms who can turn themselves into almost anything, but their natural state is a liquid protoplasm and they link together forming the community named Great Link. The *Human Instrumentality Project* may aim at the future of humanity evolving into shape-shifting species from present humanoid form. In the Changeling community, everyone is in liquid form connecting together and there is no separate individuality. In the storyline of Evangelion, Gendo Ikari and his colleagues had a conviction that evolving to the status like Changelings is the only chance for humanity to survive. In StarTrek Universe, Changelings were also humanoid species with solid forms in the remote past, but who evolve into shape shifters out of necessity.

It also serves as a metaphor of ideological objectives of totalitarian regimes like Nazi Germany, pre-Second World War Japan dominated by Shinto based nationalism in the 20th century or North Korea in the 21st century. Particularly, it appears to be an allegory and satire of Japan's State Shinto prior to the Second World War, which taught that the entire nation must become one spiritual and organic entity named *Kokutai* or "sacred national body" under the supreme reign of the Divine Emperor. Gendo was a sincere and dedicated person to his ideology for a better world like General Hideki Tojo (1884 – 1948) who forced the entire nation of Japan to comply with what he had believed. Gendo, with no doubt of his belief, forced his own son Shinji and other youngsters to dedicate themselves to the "greater good" in which he believed. During the Second World War, many Japanese had the same attitude as Gendo or Tojo and taught their youth the noblest cause is total dedication and sacrifice for the realization of a better world. Many parents of those days had no hesitation to send their sons to the battle field or even as members of *Kamikaze Party* or *AIchida* like suicide attack squad crushing themselves into US aircraft carriers. They did so because they firmly believed that their sons were becoming *kami* or Shinto deities after dying for the emperor of whom they were extremely proud.

At the end of the movie *The End of Evangelion*, Lilith/Rei collapsed in the same way as No Face in Miyazaki's Spirited Away and returned into the original form before ending the world when the toxic Human Instrumentality Project failed. The movie also illustrates well the way the real historical monster named *Kokutai* or the national body of Imperial Japan, which grew like Lilith/Rei, continuing to swallow or simulate live human bodies and souls until it finally fell apart. When the Imperial Japan was defeated, Kokutai was dismantled by the commanders of Allied Force and individual Japanese citizens obtained their freedom to live separately with their own autonomy in the same way as the end of *Lilith/Rei* and *No Face*, allowing separate beings to come back into existence.

Religion

The religious symbolism in Neon Genesis Evangelion is eclectic, and taken from many faiths around the world. But the most prominent symbolism takes its inspiration from Judeo-Christian sources and frequently uses iconography and themes from Judaism and Christianity. Nevertheless, the Evangelion also incorporates pagan symbols from Gnosticism, and Kabbalism, in the series' examination of religious ideas and themes.

Assistant director Kazuya Tsurumaki said that they originally used Christian symbolism only to give the project a unique edge against other giant robot shows, and that it had no particular meaning, and was meant to be susceptible to multiple interpretations. Hiroki Sato, head of Gainax's PR department, has made similar statements. According to Sato, references, with multiple equally plausible interpretations, include: Adam and Eve (known in other languages as Eva), the first human beings from the book of Genesis. Evas are clones Adam (except Unit 01 which came from Lilith) in the same way as Eve comes from his rib. Similarly, the Eva models come from the Angel first identified as Adam. The Christian cross is often shown, frequently represented by energy beams shooting up skyward.

In some Jewish folklore, Lilith the second Angel is the queen of the demons and the first wife of Adam, and in some works of popular culture, the first vampire. She had been one of the wives of Sammael, one of important archangels in Talmudic and post-Talmudic lore who later rebelled against God, becoming the Angel of Death. But of a wild, heroic and passionate nature, she left her spouse and joined Adam. Lilith, like Adam, had been created from the dust of the earth. But as soon as she had joined Adam they began to quarrel, each refusing to be subservient and submissive to the other. According to the legend, "I am your lord and master," spoke Adam, "and it is your duty to obey me." But Lilith replied: "We are both equal, for we are both issued from dust, and I will not be submissive to you." And thus they quarreled and neither would give in. When Lilith saw this she spoke the Ineffable Name of the Creator and soared up into the air. Thereupon Adam stood in prayer before the Creator and thus he spake: "O Lord of the Universe, the woman Thou hast given me has fled from me." [99]

In another legend, Lilith is impaled with a spear named the

---

99   Angelo S. Rappoport. The Story Of Lilith: from Ancient Israel: Myths and Legends. Was available September 2008: http://www.lilitu.com/lilith/rappoport.html

"Lance of Longinus", used to pierce the side of Jesus during his crucifixion. The legend of Lilith and the message of the three angels is found in several sources of Rabbinical lore in some of which it is quoted from the *Alphabetum Siracidis*. In these Jewish Extra-Biblical, Rabbinical lore, Lilith represents the first woman and mother of humanity and traditionally she is identified as being the mother of all demons (who are called in general the "Lilin" or "Lilim"). In Evangelion, she may even be the source of humanity itself, as Kaworu the last angel with human form says; he identifies Lilith as the source of the Lilim (humanity) in episode 24, "The Final Angel."

In the Bible, the Book of Isaiah 34:14, describing the desolation of Edom, is the only occurrence of Lilith. The scripture reads, "The wild beasts of the desert shall also meet with the wild beasts of the island, and the satyr shall cry to his fellow; the screech owl also shall rest there, and find for herself a place of rest" (KJV). This passage refers to God's day of vengeance, when the land will be transformed into desolate wilderness. Thus, Lilith was known in ancient Israel of the 8th century BC. The fact that she found a place of rest in the desert from this passage seems to allude to the Sumerian Gilgamesh incident: after Lilith fled into the desert, she apparently found repose there.

The Angels could be a reference to the angels of God from the Old Testament, the word used is the same one used for apostle (or messenger), as in the New Testament during the series as well as the introduction sequence flashes "Angels" at one point. In addition, their origin is vaguely explained in the series as descending from "Adam" (yet another Judeo-Christian reference) and being "different evolutionary paths humanity could have taken."

The Magi supercomputers are named Melchior, Balthasar and Casper after the names traditionally given for the Magi who were mentioned in the Gospel of Matthew as having visited Jesus in Bethlehem (often called "the three wise men", though the number of visitors is not recorded in the Gospel).

The Tree of Sephiroth (Tree of Life) is mentioned, as well as shown in the opening title sequence and on the ceiling of Gendo's office, with Hebrew inscriptions on it (the terms written there are mostly Kabbalic).

The Marduk Institute is an anime front organization for NERV, tasked with finding the teenagers suitable for piloting Evangelion units. Marduk was the name of the chief Babylonian deity and patron god of the city of Babylon.

In episode 9, Asuka describes the door between her and Shinji as the "Wall of Jericho" which, in the Book of Joshua, was an impenetrable wall, though it eventually fell after being circled seven times by the army and priests of Israel.

Reference is made to the "Room of Gaff" (spelling taken from the English subtitles; correct spelling/transliteration is "Guf") and its being "empty." In some Jewish lore outside of the Old Testament, when the *Room of Gaff* is emptied of souls waiting to be born, the end of the world, and with it the coming of the Messiah, is nigh. It is a similar concept as "the pre-existence of souls" in Mormon religion. Anno also linked this concept with the popular idea of reincarnation or transmigration of souls coming from Buddhism, since Judaism does not hold that souls transmigrate.

The *Room of Gaff* is further referenced in *Death and Rebirth* and *End of Evangelion*, where it is given greater importance than just one mention in the television series. One analysis of the End of Evangelion has it being "the door to both the beginning and the end of the world, and the hall of souls. When exposed to the power of the *Hall of Gaff* all living forms lose their ability to maintain themselves as individual life forms, reverting to LCL. At the Second Impact the door to the Hall of Gaff is opened by Adam, and everything changes into a sea of LCL. At the Third Impact the portal is opened once again by Rei, who has assimilated with Lilith, and all life-forms revert to LCL." Note that in the movies, human souls come from and return to the Hall of Gaff. There seems to be two separate Rooms of Gaff in the movies: one for the humans, openable through Lilith in the Japanese GeoFront; and a different one, presumably for the Angels in the Antarctic GeoFront, which was opened on the same day the Second Impact occurred. The angels themselves are named after angels from angelology, including Sachiel, Shamshel, and Arael.

Quang Truong (2008) maintained that the Neon Genesis Evangelion was created based on the pagan philosophical assumption, although author/director Hideaki Anno incorporated Judeo-Christian religious symbolism to his work. Truong contends,

Some people have pinned it on religion as the reason why the Japanese are so much more quick to adapt to and be comfortable with technology; because their native religion, Shinto, attributes a living spirit to all objects in the world. This is as opposed to Judeo-Christians, who believe that Judeo-Christians, who believe that humans are distinct from and fundamentally different from everything else (2008).

He viewed that the Neon Genesis Evangelion is based on Shinto based spirituality rather than Judeo-Christians religiosity. Therefore, the bio-mechanical angels resembles Shinto Kami and God Warrior from Hayao Miyazaki's *Nausicaä of the Valley of the Wind* (1984) although they were named after Jewish angelology.

On the other hand, Redmond (2007) states that Anno's

primary focus was secular and socio-political in nature, although he used variety of religious symbolisms. According to Redmond,

Although Anno quotes from a wide variety of mystical, religious and theological texts, symbols and icons in the course of the series, ranging from Shintoism, Buddhism, Christianity, Islam, and several varieties of mysticism, Anno has a decidedly secular purpose in mind here. The gospel in question is not a religion per se, but a globe-spanning belief system which has certain characteristics of an organized religion, but which is primarily concerned with the control of technology and human labor-power (2007).

Redmond also argued that the Anno's symbolisms could be inspired by the ones Hayao Miyazaki employed. He argued that Miyazaki built on the trope of Asiazilla in that powerful symbol of an ecological or proto-East Asian collectivity, the "Shishigami" or Forest Spirit of Princess Mononoke (1997) and the River-Spirit of Spirited Away (2001) — the rewriting of the bio-mechanical God-warriors or Ohmu of Miyazaki's manga Nausicaa into one of Anno's humanized Evangelions. The statement of Misato Katsuragi, "Bath is a laundry of life" in the second episode also indicates the Shinto based philosophy of Hideaki Anno, because cleansing ritual with water is an extremely important part of Shintoism. A Shinto priest takes baths to cleanse themselves and wash their hands before worshiping in a shrine, since physical cleanness is extremely important in Shinto religion. It is also known that many Shinto Kami or deities favour bathing. The motif of Shinto deities having baths could be observed in Miyazaki's Spirited Away. Various Shinto Kami gathers in Yubaba's bathhouse where Chihiro works in order to clean themselves or do the "laundry of life."

Finally, the brand of beer "Yebisu Beer" that Misato favors

could indicate Anno's Shinto inclination, because "Yebisu" or "Hiruko no Mikoto" is one of Japan's Seven Lucky Gods. He is a very significant Shinto deity, the god of good fortune, the ocean, and fishing folk. The smiling and bearded Ebisu is most often depicted dressed as a Japanese peasant with a fishing rod in his right hand, and with a large red sea bream. Hiruko is also known for his tragic upbringing as the third son of the Shinto gods Izanagi-no-Mikoro and Izanami-no-Mikoto, the progenitors of the islands of Japan. Yet since he was born without any bones he was cast out into the ocean at age three. As he grew up, he overcome his physical handicap and became a god of the sea and fisheries. Japanese developed a beer named after Yebisu in the 19th century since he was the god of fisheries. In the context of Evangelion, Yebisu or Hiruko no Mikoto as a god of the sea might parallel with the theme of mother like Evas with amniotic fluid within and the Human Instrumentality Project that all mankind are connected to each other within the ocean of life.

Are they Fallen Angels?

One question that could be raised of the Neon Genesis Evangelion Is, are these the fallen angels? They are hostile to humans and trying to wipe them out from the earth like demons in the Devilman. From Judeo-Christian tradition, the attitude toward the humanity is one of vital criteria to determine whether certain angels are good or bad, because man is created in the image of God. Although humans are a little lower than angels themselves, the position of mankind in the creation order is secured in Genesis 1:28. It means God does not allow angels to slaughter humans in the same way as we slaughter food animals. If they do, it means that they are rebelling against his order because men are as important as angels from the biblical perspectives. However, as Truong noted, Anno the author has no concept of the creation order. He views mankind as the same as all other creatures on earth and in the universe. Angels are life forms higher and more intelligent than mankind. Since pagan perspectives including Shinto do not give a special place to humanity in the creation order, they give higher beings like angels permission to treat humans in the same way as the rest of creation. Many of us consume meat from slaughtered fish, avian, four-legged mammals and sometimes even reptiles. Those who believe in evolutionism view monkeys as very similar to mankind genetically or even related to them. However, it is said that few in South East Asia enjoy the delicacy of the monkey meat and brain. In modern and civilized society, cruelty to animals is not considered an honorable conduct. In most advanced nations a cruel act to animals is punishable as a misdemeanor or minor felony with a range from a fine to short prison sentence. It does not, however, make the violator equal to a serial killer, mass murderer or war criminal.

In the same way, it is OK for angels to consume our meat or even eliminate us as pest animals from the Shinto/pagan perspective or any worldview outside of the Judeo-Christian tradition. Bio-mechanical angels from the Neon Genesis Evangelion and demons from Devilman are extremely cruel and hostile to the humanity. But this does not qualify them as "fallen" angels unless the story is written from the Judeo-Christian perspective. From the pagan perspective, angels who slaughter and devour live human beings are not considered rebellious angels or demons, in the same way men who butcher and eat everything in the animal realm are not labeled as a criminal against humanity.

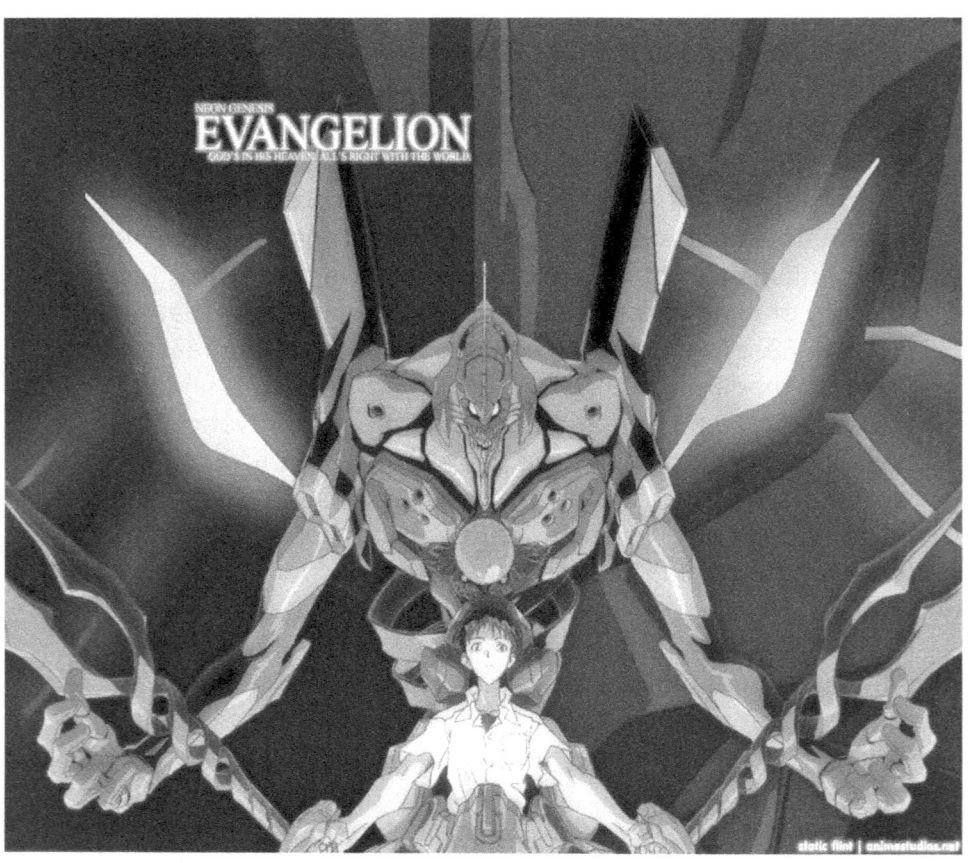

[100]Hideaki Anno. Neon Genesis Evangelion. Hyjoo.com, 2003.[101]

---

100 Was available May 2009: http://www.hyjoo.com/sujet-11579.html
101 The picture is used under "fair dealing" (Canada) and "fair use" (USA) provisions in copyright law.

6

Conclusion (Otaku Manifesto)

Otaku & Annihilation of Cultural Boundaries

The new culture centered around Japanese animation and comics called Otaku was dispersed all over the globe after the 1990s and became a highly popular item among youth and young adults world-wide. In terms of the dispersion of Japanese animation, Toshiya Ueno (1996) cited:

"Japanimation is traveling through the cultural diaspora into the world, and is translated, communicated, and misunderstood. The passage from Donna Haraway's 'A Cyborg Manifesto' should be cited: "There is no way to read the following list from a standpoint of "identification" of a unitary self. The issue is dispersion. The task is to survive in the diaspora." If the image of shell and suit in cyborg has been moving, it is not vain to discover the "automated other" in various expressions and in global information capitalism itself. It is another way to "animate" the other and the minority."

The emergence and diaspora of Otaku culture is well paralleled to the advent of globalization and the two phenomena are vital forces to demolish national and ethnic-cultural boundaries. Kumiko Sato (2007) contends that perhaps a more disturbing problem for scholars of Japanese literature and culture is that what one says about Japan is no longer about 'Japan'. Today's cultural boundaries are increasingly eroding, as ethnic and cultural differences are no longer invented through exports and imports across national borders as in the modern era. Rather, in the post-modern era, they are produced by the acts of consumption in which one participates. In other words, we live in the era in which the term "culture" is going to divorce from both state-nations in the modern era and ethnicity. This ultimate divorce enables every individual person to choose and live his or her own personal and private culture no matter what kind of ethnicity to which he or she belongs.

Several recent scholarly publications, such as Koichi Iwabuchi's *Recentering Globalization: Popular Culture and Japanese Transnationalism* (2002) and Anne Allison's *Millennial Monsters: Japanese Toys and the Global Imagination* (2006), examine the globalization and localization of Japanese culture through the marketing of anime, video games and other similar products. They look specifically at how the business of configuring Japanese identity through the relationship between culture and technology will undergo changes expected from this gradual erasure of differences between culture and technology. One of the pressing questions for Japanologists is how the indigenousness of the culture persists while the dominance of technology contintues to define culture advances.

Summarizing Ueno's and Sato's statement, the anime and Otaku culture was dispersed just as the era of globalization arrived, becoming a popular entertainment item in a globalized community without cultural boundaries. Some animes have the story settings of near future with no national and cultural boundaries so that national and ethnic identities become mere fossils or relics. Otaku culture is also characterized with the post-modern view that has abandoned a typical modernistic discourse to follow a story line in linear fashion.

In this, we go back to William Gibson's definition of Otakuhood that Otaku prefer data to objects and are post-national and extra-geographical. Otakuhood is a culture of Web, in which all are curators of his or her own personal space, or museum, and are typically post-modern.

Spiritual Dimension of Otaku Culture

The spiritual components of anime and manga world are characterized by their eclecticism from numerous options. It is due to the Japanese history that they have been comfortable with holding a multiplicity of spiritual beliefs. Buddhism, Confucianism and Christianity were all introduced to the population of the archipelago within the past two millennia and ingested to varying degrees. Anime and Manga culture has inherited the unique cohabitation of the multiplicity of beliefs from the land. It also possesses a rich soil of spiritual dimension, having embraced various spiritualities from all over the world besides Japanese indigenous spirituality. It is like the Pantheon of the gods of Ancient Rome, or a "spiritual expo" in which viewers can observe some Judeo-Christian components, Western paganism and mythologies, the Buddhism that immigrated to Japan nearly 2000 years ago and Shinto, one of the few surviving animistic faiths in the world and the most archaic in Japan existing from the pre-literal era.

Folklore & Romanticism

Dr. Alwyn Spies teaches Japanese pop-culture including anime and manga as well as the Japanese language at UBC Okanoagan in Kelowna, British Columbia, Canada. She has offered a course on Japanese pop-culture in English since 2008. Her course proved extremely popular and the enrollment soared to 75 in the first semester. She also offers content-based Japanese language courses using well-known manga as text books, and these also have high enrollments. However, the university administration has not always been supportive to her enterprise to teach Otaku culture. She agrees that North American adults are quite unaware of anime and manga culture, as it came from Japan less than two decades ago, and many are opposed to this new trend among youth and young adults. When Dr. Spies first offered a Japanese pop-culture course and Japanese language courses using manga materials as text books, the administration was skeptical that her courses would have sufficient enrollment.

Many westerners from the older generation often have a tremendous misconception that anime or all animated movies are "cartoons" or "kids stuff". They disregard these materials as not serious enough to be discussed as an academic topic. Eri Izawa (1997), however, maintains that the contemporary anime and manga culture has developed from the rich soil and tradition of Japanese classic and modern fantasy literatures, folklore and romanticism created millennia ago. These are almost completely foreign to the vast majority of westerners, unless they are students of classic Japanese literature. Izawa contends that:

Romanticism in Japan is hardly new or unusual, and is found in many media. The Lady Murasaki, who lived at the turn of the millennium, is reknowned for having written what may have been the world's first full novel, the Tale of Genji, rich in poetic emotion and imagery. Though the feudal years pushed the arts into the background of Japanese thought, historic figures like the tragic warlord Yoshitsune were eventually

Conclusion (Otaku Manifesto)

touched by a legendary, Arthurian edge. In the meantime, Japanese folklore remained rich with fairy tales of fantastic creatures, ghosts, and monsters, aided by belief in gods and spirits from Shinto and Buddhism, and given depth by Taoism. Even World War II era Japan, geared up for war and battle, fell in love with "romantic" music about soldiers' experiences in China. [102]

Izawa notes that many Westerners hold the stereotypical image of Japanese people as a cold, calculating land of ant-like workers, brutal efficiency and overwhelming bureaucracy in which individual wills are suppressed by the collective and corporate will. She argues this is due to the economical and business oriented sides of the nation having been introduced to the West in the past several decades in the "pre-otaku" modernist era. However, as Izawa maintains, the romantic, imaginative and often individualistic, side almost to the degree of egotism among the population of this archipelago, has existed over a millennium.

Many westerners perhaps see Japan as the land in which any kind of individualism is not permitted and where there is little room for passionate and romantic loves. Historically, romantic loves and intimate relationships that did not serve the collective good were strongly discouraged. This is why Japan and most East Asian areas carry the tradition of "arranged marriages." Western critics may parallel this lack of individualism as "the Borg collective" in the StarTrek Universe. However, Izawa argues that the *Tale of Genji*[103], written by Lady Murasaki Shikibu[104], demonstrates romantic love among the ancient Japanese and suggests some different individualism

---

102 Eri Izawa. The Romantic, Passionate Japanese in Anime: A Look at the Hidden Japanese Soul: Japan Pop! Inside the World of Japanese Popular Culture, 1997.

103 Wikepedia: The Tale of Genji. Was available April 2009: http://en.wikipedia.org/wiki/The_Tale_of_Genji

104 Wikepedia: Murasaki Shikibu. Was available April 2009: http://en.wikipedia.org/wiki/Murasaki_Shikibu

from the West has existed in Japan over a millennia. Other romantic and tragic tales are centered around Minamoto no Yoshitsune (1159 – 1189), a general of the Minamoto clan of Japan in the late Heian and early Kamakura period. [105]

In addition, Japanese folklores written prior to the *Tale of Genji* describe romantic heroes such as *Yamato Takeru,* a Japanese legendary warrior prince whose soul turns into a great white bird and flies away after his death. This demonstrates romantic loves, individual struggles, tragic destinies, themes centered around death, afterlife and the spiritual world. [106] Yamato Takeru is remembered as one of several archetypes of a romantic hero throughout the history, and many anime and manga heroes today are loosely modeled after him. In her article, Izawa argues that the Tale of Genji, tragic stories about the warlord Minamoto no Yoshitsune, and folklores centered on the Prince Yamato Takeru exhibit a more passionate and individualistic side of the nation of which most westerners were unaware.

Individualistic philosophies did not grow as in the West on Japanese soil likely because of the Confucianism that came from China during the second and third century. It played a major role to suppress individualism among the Japanese. It taught the island nation to kill a "small insect" or an individual to sustain a "larger insect" or a community over and over throughout the history. However, the Confucian philosophy failed to eradicate or completely annihilate individualism among the nation, and some rebel factors popped out from time to time. In the level of popular literatures and folklore, Japanese loves romantic heroes with individualistic mindset. And the ways of life of these heroes have become the archetypes and a vital part of the collective unconscious among the island nation.

---

105 Wikepedia: Minamoto no Yoshitsune. Was available April 2009: http://en.wikipedia.org/wiki/Minamoto_no_Yoshitsune

106 Wikepedia: Yamato Takeru. Was available April 2009: http://en.wikipedia.org/wiki/Yamato_Takeru

The stereotypical image of Japanese that was introduced to the West and the rest of the world as android or ant-like workers, was during the modernist era after the Meiji Restoration. This was a revolution, a chain of events that led to enormous changes in Japan's political and social structure in the 19th century. Now, however, this image is being replaced by a new picture following the "Otaku-Diaspora". The dispersion of anime and manga based culture has taken place during the past two decades as a post-modernist phenomenon that has exposed several different aspects of the nation and their culture and traditions. The hero archetypes regarding Japanese have now been transferred into the global community and are rapidly becoming a part of the global collective unconscious.

Shinto Motif & Nature – Hayao Miyazaki

Anime makers such as Hayao Miyazaki clearly express the Shinto motif and worldview in their works. Many Miyazaki characters are modeled after kami or deities and heroes from Japanese mythology from Kojiki, the oldest Japanese literature in written form and some other archaic writings. These characters and the natural world in Miyazaki's films express an underlying belief of the early Shinto worldview and theme, dealing with the relationship between humanity and nature. He describes the spiritual world as existing in the same domain as the physical world. Unlike the Western worldview, the ancient Japanese did not precisely demarcate their world into the material and the spiritual, nor between this world and another perfect world to come.

According to Lucy Wright (2005), the framework of "the Ancient Way", one of the most important philosophical assumptions in Miyazaki's work, was developed by eighteenth century Kojiki scholar Moto-ori Norinaga (1730-1801). His philosophy has been used as the most influential and detailed codification of the early form of natural Shinto. Wright contends that both Norinaga and Miyazaki are nostalgically seeking contact with the "pure" mystical core of this belief system, but with very different outcomes. She argues that:

Norinaga's ideas informed the kokugaku (National Studies) movement, which eventually led to the ideology of Tennoism and to Japan's imperialist expansion program in the nineteenth and twentieth centuries. Miyazaki attempts to distance himself from the significant political and nationalistic implications inherent in any discussion of Shinto, and yet is still drawing on the cultural myth of an idealised, paradisal existence in ancient Japan. But where Norinaga and others of the Nativist school considered the magokoro of ancient times to be a Japanese birthright, Miyazaki's vision is more expansive and global. His characters can be described as both "performing Japaneseness" but also exemplifying foreign cultural traits that coalesce into coherent and transnational human traits.

So although Norinaga and Miyazaki shared the same essence Shinto based philosophy and "the spirit of Japaneseness", they moved in completely different directions. Norinaga's philosophy was used as the basis of the ideology of the emperor cult and Japan's imperialist expansion program in the 19th and 20th centuries long after his death. Miyazaki, however, successfully managed to globalize the same core of "Japanese spirit" as Norinaga and the concept of *magokoro* or "sincere heart" of ancient times.

Thus, this innovative introduction of the "Japanese spirit" to the rest of the world endorsed Miyazaki as a new spiritual guru and a teacher of environmentalism. He appears to be boldly propagating the new philosophy to the global community, particularly the West. Western viewers tired of Western rationalism, dualism and materialism seem to sympathize with his views. Some even view Miyazaki as a Messiah like figure who saves the world from the environmental pollutions in the physical domain and as a proponent of the philosophy of enlightenment in the spiritual domain.

Ironically, over a half century ago, the entire nation of Japan was driven into the madness of the emperor cult and to an imperialist expansion program based on the similar philosophical assumption of the spirit of Japaneseness based on Shinto naturalism. Therefore Miyazaki's greatness lays in the fact that he managed to modify, remodel and globalize the concept of "Japanese spirit" or the philosophical assumption that was never accepted by the global society in the previous century.

Leiji Matsumoto & Horoscope/ Taoism gods in the sky

Leiji Matsumoto seemingly adopted themes of horoscope spirituality and Taoism gods in the sky since most story settings of his works take place in space. In Taoism, many deities like Jade Emperor, the Mother Empress of the West, the Mother of the Bushel of Stars and the Seven Star Lords of the Northern Bushel reside in space and administrate the destiny of mankind and all other creatures. For the ancient Chinese, space was the theatre of fantasy, romance, myth or any colorful and imaginative stories. Izawa (1997) contends that ancient China is a land of enchantment, the Eastern equivalent of Western high fantasy; handsome people in beautiful clothing, spectacular magic, strange monsters, and fascinating legends. Likewise, Matsumoto created a "romantic" world projected to space full of handsome people in beautiful clothing and strange monsters and aliens.

In Taoism, Jade Emperor is the highest deity who resides in space and overseees the fate and destiny of all creations of the universe. Matsumoto also postulates the same assumption about super-natural beings who reside in space. For him, outer space is the stage for romance and tragedy and fantastic adventure, in which the taste of heroism, passionate love, personal struggle, and eternal longing for power and immortality are the main themes. In the theatre of space, according to Matsumoto, both natural and super-natural activities are happening on a daily basis and control people's lives. In his works, Matsumoto also displays the underlying philosophical assumption to value mortality over immortality and free will rather than fixed destiny.

His preference of mortality to immortality seems to agree with Homer's ancient Greek *Iliad* and the *Odyssey*. Matsumoto seems to have the same theme as Homer who describes woes and miseries coming from immortal bodies made of machines and an extremely long life, such as Achilles as opposed to the immortal Apollo.

Devilman, Demons & Theme of Anti-war

Devilman is based on Nagai's fascination with the Judeo-Christian world and probably his most well-known and philosophically deep creation. It has the same level of philosophical depth as John Milton's *Paradise Lost* and Johann Wolfgang von Goethe's *Faust* dealing with existential anguish of both men and rebellious angels. Many manga and anime critics argue that the major theme of Devilman is anti-war and Nagai himself has admitted it. The story of Akira Fudo who joined the demon Amon to protect mankind from legions of demons, might indicate a powerful nation state on earth that takes up a weapon of mass destruction embarks on war to protect itself and allies and the "entire humanity" from demons in their own mind'.

For some viewers, the image of Akira might parallel the former U.S. President George W. Bush who embarked on the war in both Afghanistan and Iraq in the name of "war on terrorism" or a battle to protect humanity from evil terrorists and evil leaders or "demons" in the Near East. When Bush was elected as the 43rd president of the United States in January 2001, he obtained the power to control and harness the mightiest military force on the planet, comparable with Amon, one of the mightiest dark angels and the Duke of Hell. Bush quoted the Bible as he was waging the war against the Taliban, Al-Qaida, Saddam Hussein's army and "demons". It appears to be a similar philosophy as "eye for eye, tooth for tooth" in Exodus 21:24 of the Old Testament. Bush and the Republicans had a strong conviction they were embarking on the war for the sake of the Kingdom of God.

Pagan Mythologies & World of Go Nagai

Go Nagai also incorporated Western pagan mythologies as well as Judeo-Christian myths into his works. He created the *Mazinger Z* with the theme of Greco-Roman Hellenism, later expanded the same theme to *Great Mazinger*, *God Mazinger* and *Mazinkaiser* in which he developed the concept of the giant mecha. *Mazinger Z* and its later spinoffs are based on his strong fascination and romanticism with the ancient Greco-Roman world. Nagai also created *UFO Robo Grendizer* based on his other romantic fantasy on Northern and Western European chivalry and myths centered on the hero Siegfried. Finally, God Mazinger is based on Nagai's romantic fascination with the ancient Shamanic world of Mu, the lost continent.

In his robot anime loosely linked with the Western pagan world, Nagai also expressed the theme of anti-war and his aversion against war particularly in *UFO Robo Grendizer*. He describes a military state in space, the Vega Empire, ruled by the dictator King Vega. The empire is badly polluted by Vegatron, a powerful radioactive substance used to produce weapons of mass destruction. Nagai describes a tragedy of an entire race or species that has sold its souls to the devil to conquer the entire Milky Way Galaxy.

His anti-war theme seems to have stemmed from his early childhood memory of the havoc the war created and his reminiscence of pre-Second World War Imperial Japan. Nagai seems to have a strong aversion against Imperial Japan, a formidable totalitarian military state that started a holy war with the rationale to save the whole of East Asia and the rest of the world. But in 1945, Imperial Japan was utterly defeated in 1945 when Nagai was born. It is easy to surmise that his memory of old Imperial Japan spawned the picture of the mighty and evil Vega Empire.

Evangelion & Biblical/Judeo Christian Symbolism

Neon Genesis Evangelion is a commercially and critically successful, influential and popular Japanese anime series that began in October 1995. The concept of Evangelion is an extension of Nagai's giant mecha series. However, unlike Nagai's robots that are generally mechanical structures, Evas are unique life-forms with both organic and robotic attributes. The concept of robotic creatures with both organic and robotic natures may be seen in "zords" in *Mighty Morphin Power Rangers* (1993) or North American made Transformers (1986/ 2007) and many recently made anime productions. The etymology of Nagai's Mazinger has a spiritual connotation as "Majin" is the combination of the Japanese words "Ma" (魔), demon, and "Jin" (神), god. However, in Nagai's stories, there is no indication that Mazingers are literally "Majin" or real gods with spiritual and biological components, since the term is more figurative and symbolic. However, Evas are biological and spiritual in a more literal sense than Nagai's Mazingers.

Evangelion is rich in allusions to biological, philosophical, religious and psychological concepts. The religious symbolism in Neon Genesis Evangelion is eclectic, and taken from many faiths around the world although main components are of Judeo Christian origin. The most prominent symbolism takes its inspiration from either Canonical or Apocryphal literatures and frequently uses iconography and themes from Judaism and Christianity. At the same time, the Evangelion incorporates symbols with loosely or heretically Judeo-Christian origins like Gnosticism, Kabbalism, and some totally pagan symbols as well. The interpretation of the symbols and concepts varies from individual to individual, and it is not clear how many are intentional or meaningful, or which are merely design elements or coincidences.

Although Hideaki Anno, the author of Evangelion, incorporates symbols from the Judeo-Christian world, his basic philosophical assumptions are predominantly Shinto and other Japanese indigenous spiritualities. For instance, the statement of Commander Misato Katsuragi, one of major characters of Eva, "Bath is a laundry of life" comes from the Shinto based philosophy. In Christianity and Judaism, there is a tradition of Baptismal ritual as an initiation ceremony to enter the faith group. It also carries the symbolism to cleanse the sins and stains of a person's life as well as the symbolism of death to sinful degenerate existence. Unlike Shinto tradition, however, water does not literally cleanse but the cleansing act requires the mighty work of God.

Unlike Judeo-Christian tradition, Shinto does not carry the concept of "sin" as an extremely obstinate ultimate dirt of life almost comparable with "karma" in Buddhism, so that any stain and shortcomings in life are actually washable in water. In the story setting, the earth has more water than today because Antarctic glaciers are totally destroyed by biomechanical "angels". It highlights the Shinto motif of "bath" and sacred water to cleanse our life. Anno also describes a water planet full of water as an allusion from the Freudian concept that our life has started in an amniotic sac from a mother's body filled with water.

The cockpit of Eva is made like a mother's amniotic sac filled with fluid called LCL (Link Connect Liquid) which synthesizes the pilot's brain and Eva's own mind. When the connection between the two is perfect, the Evangelion is mighty and formidable. If not, it is easily destroyed by the "angels". At the end of the series, the Human Instrumentality Project, one of the main themes of the whole narrative is revealed. All human beings are connected to each other through LCL. The project reduces all humans to LCL, or "primordial soup," the fundamental composite of human beings. All LCL would then be united into a supreme being, the next stage of humanity, ending all conflict, loneliness and pain brought about by individual existence. The earth in the series became a water-full planet as the result of the angel's attack on the Antarctica. Then, this earth is turned into a planet of "great link" in which all humans are interconnected through a massive amniotic sac.

The conversion of the earth into a planet filled with water like a massive amniotic sac a in mother's womb might parallel with the advent of so called Era of Aquarius or the constellation of a massive urn filled with water. The predecessor of this era is Era of Pisces or the constellation of twin fish, which might symbolize the masculinity, penis, perpetual aggression and conflicts, Imperialism, faith in endless progress of mankind, the philosophy of enlightenment and modernity. It is often wrongly identified as the era of Christianity because "fish" is also a symbol of Christ and Greek acronym of "Christ Jesus Our Lord and Savior". On the other hand, Aquarius or a massive urn in the space is considered as a symbol of feminity, vagina, inclusiveness vs. exclusiveness, absence of conflicts, post-modernity and globalism.

Otaku & Christianity

From an evangelical Christian perspective, it might be beneficial to pay attention to the following two areas with respect to Otaku or a new cultural global reach through anime and manga. First, is Otaku culture totally against Christian principles or carrying any indication of Anti-Christ who is supposed to come in the end time? Second, is there any Judeo-Christian cultural and religious influence in the Otakudom or any part of Otaku impacted by Christianity? Third, is it possible to build a bridge between Christianity and the newer generation influenced by Otakudom, so that we can start a missiological dialogue with them?

For the first question, I will say an absolute "no". I am aware that many Christians strongly disapprove of the manga and anime materials because they contain sexual promiscuity, homosexuality, and extreme violence. In fact, anime and manga narratives deal with many themes that contradict the values of Christianity. But this raises another question. Do we see all these pornographic and violent items only in the newly developed genres of graphic novel or entertainment? Of course, the answer is, "no". Pornography has an extremely long history and possibly existed in the era before any writing systems existed in the world. Almost all modern and pre-modern nation states produced literature classified as "pornography". Christian scholars of literature today study some novels with sexually provocative descriptions like *Lady Chatterley's Lovers* (1928) written by D.H. Laurence (1885 – 1930) and write academic theses and articles focused on the philosophical depth of the author. Laurence is known as a follower of the school called "Philosophy of Life" who regards the entire universe as a massive "sea of life", from which all living beings are coming from by birth and returning to upon death. He describes the sexuality as a significant event in the "sea of life". Christian scholars and literary critics will not agree with his philosophy because it is basically paganism and similar to Hinduism in supporting the idea of "reincarnation", yet they might find it worthwhile to study.

Should we reject or refuse to read this literature simply because they are "pornographic" or immoral? Should we ban all Christian youth and young adults from reading novels written by Laurence because his philosophy is similar to Eastern animism and paganism? If we do so, in effect, the entire Christian community would slip into the literary Dark Ages. Is there any difference between D.H. Laurence's *Lady Chatterley's Lovers* and anime and manga products with sexual overtones like Go Nagai's *Devilman*? As I have mentioned in Chapter 4, Devilman contains many nudities, scenes of violence and grotesque and gruesome descriptions of battles and massacres. However, *Devilman* is one of best masterpieces with philosophical depth through which readers can learn the way Japanese understand demons in the Judeo-Christian traditions. To conclude, both traditional literatures and manga/anime can be equally moral or immoral, philosophically deep or shallow and subjects of academic studies.

As for the second question, I will safely say "yes" to this question. Otaku culture is very eclectic and multifaceted in nature because it has incorporated various cultures and religiosities on earth, in the same way as Japan has vigorously acquired the knowledge and technologies from the rest of the world, particularly the West after the Meiji Restoration (1868). Because of this, there is also a Judeo-Christian influence in the Anime and Manga culture. Sabrina Surovec (2002) said, "When Westerners watch anime for the first time, they are often struck by what seem to be random uses of Judeo-Christian religious elements." She also stated that the concept of angels and demons were introduced to anime, as well as the use of "Western" religious symbols and Judeo-Christian symbolism like the cross and the Star of David as well as pagan

Conclusion (Otaku Manifesto)

symbolism like pentagrams, hexagrams, etc. As prolific anime and manga authors having created a globally based new culture, these artists have also incorporated Judeo-Christian components into their works either consciously or unconsciously. For instance, *Devilman* by Go Nagai and *Neon Genesis Evangelion* by Hideaki Anno will amaze the viewers with the richness and depth of the world of demons and fallen angels coming from Judeo-Christian myths and demonologies based on both canonical and apocryphal or heretical narratives.

Having absorbed and incorporated various cultures and spirituality, the Otakudom grew into an important part of the global culture. We can safely conclude that Otaku culture already declared independence from Japan, and abandoned the status to be simply a sub-culture of the Japanese.

Regarding the third question whether one can build a bridge between Christianity and Otakudom, I will also say "yes." From a Christian perspective, there is one optimistic factor that some components from a Christian heritage are still alive and relevant in anime and otaku culture. As it comes from the post modern era, it would be crucial let go of the mindset coming modern era of emphasis on man's intellectual ability and the potency of natural science. The Modernist tends to see all things in the universe in black and white and reject all grays or ambiguity. Although modernism is essentially a secular humanism apart from the Christian tradition, it has sneaked into the Christendom in the West and impacted numerous Christian intellectuals and theologians. Modernist theologians tend to regard all human histories as linear, our universe as a closed entity with almost no room for a divine intervention, although they accept the supernatural and miracles in their metaphysical domain. They also require scientific rationale to any phenomena in the universe and reject the premise that God has reserved his ultimate right to violate all laws of the natural science.

From the traditional modernist perspective, reaching out to those in Otaku Culture is an overwhelmingly huge missiological challenge, because Otaku has a completely different mindset from the older generation of any traditional culture or ethnicity with a modernist mentality. The Otaku generation does not think science has absolute value, or see everything in the world in black and white and or view the entire universe as linear as those with modernist influence. Therefore, they do not reject the possibility of "time travel", "dimensional shifting", or moving from present reality to a different reality as described in some science fiction.

Christian theologians from post-modernist Otaku generation in the future may boldly postulate the theory that God has created the universe with multiple realities and multiple time lines. It is beyond the context of modernist thinking that follows the Enlightenment tradition. Many Modernist theologians in the theologically conservative camp have incorporated Christian orthodoxy with modernist thinking. Although the so called "neo-orthodox" theologians were responsible to allow the Enlightenment philosophy enter the Christian community, it also helped theologians to think like scholars, yet stay within the boundary of Christian Orthodoxy, in the same way as Apostle Paul who employed Greek or Hellenistic thinking of the first century when he was preaching the Gospel to the population in the Greco-Roman world. Likewise, there might be a way to incorporate Otaku and post-modernist thinking with Christian fundamentals. The post-modern "neo-neo orthodox" scholars may be open to the possibility of "time travel", "dimensional" and "reality shifting." However, there is no room for some concepts apparently coming from pagan philosophy like "the reincarnation" or the transmigration of souls, and sexual conducts like polygamy, homosexuality and incest. As we move from Piscean to Aquarian Christianity, we may eliminate wrong fish or modernism from the pond, but retain the right fish or core of Christianity.

Also, extending Surovec's logic, reaching out and starting a dialogue with the Otaku generation is not as difficult as the older generation may think because of Christian components already transferred into the *Otakudom* from the old soil. Thus, Anime and Manga with Christian components like Devilman and Evangelion could be utilized as apologetic and missiological tools to start a dialogue with Otaku.

It is not impossible to build a bridge between Christianity and the newer generation including Otaku, although there is considerable challenge. It requires study and vigorous research on the topic of Otaku culture.

A Final Challenge

So what is the ultimate social impact of the phenomena of Otaku Diaspora or the spread of the anime and manga culture to the world? It is disseminating a driving force that hopes to create a completely new and great era. Otaku had a humble beginning as a mere sub-culture of Japanese youth and young adult obsessed with anime and comics that did not carry positive connotations. But now it is a universal and collective brain power eminent among all mankind promoting global corporations and industries, new world economy and the creation of a new trans-national and trans-ethnic culture, ready to end national and ethnic boundaries and throw out nationally or ethnically based old world cultures, stereotypes and even modern nation states.

We live in a transient and rapidly changing world. There is an old Arab proverb "Dogs bark, but the caravan goes on, that is, "Life goes on, even if some will try to stop or talk against progress". Japanese modified this proverb into "Dogs bark, but history progresses". Both Arab and Japanese sayings indicate that if we try to stop or divert history and the stream of time our creator designed, we are as powerless as our four legged canine friends. Therefore, we must be "shrewd as serpents and innocent as doves" (Matthew 10:16) when we evaluate changes around us and cope with them. At the same time, we must be always keen and astute to the word of God, particularly any specific message addressed to those who live in today's world.

That astuteness reminds us that we live in post-modernity in which the Otaku generation is a driving force to change the world. We need the awareness that changes are going to happen as inevitable facts and realities, and they may be either friendly or unfriendly to us.

The impact of this is to understand that God has prepared a different message to the post-modern world and its people than to those of the modern world and the older generation. So therefore we need a different hermeneutic, or interpretational science, from the previous era. We have a call to understand the message of God correctly as directed to today's world and younger generation who live there. It is the study of anime and manga culture, that is, the thinking way of the Otaku generation, that will give a strong insight as to God's message to the post-modern world.

We are all travelers when we cross the boundaries of geographic regions or time. If we immigrate to a different region of the earth, we have to cross geographic cultures. Those who were born in the mid 20th century and are alive in the 21st century have travelled from modernity to post-modernity and across chronological cultures just as travelers can cross geographic and cultural boundaries.

The challenge is to understand fully the world around you and, rather than dismiss it, embrace its reality and interact with subcultures in a way they can understand.

Conclusion (Otaku Manifesto) 199

For manga and anime, that is to see a vision for the world that breaks down boundaries that come between people. This is great place to start as it's something Christians can embrace.

[107]Leiji Matsumoto. Space Battleship Yamato. Rbbtoday. com, 1977.[108]

---

107 Was available May 2009: http://rbbtoday.com
108 The picture is used under "fair dealing" (Canada) and "fair use" (USA) provisions in copyright law.

Dr. Ebihara's love of art came from his late mother, Ayako Ebihara, to whom this book is dedicated. This painting is her work, although grayscale cannot possibly convey the beautiful colors in the original. The full color rendering can be viewed on www.facebook.com/Isao Ebihara

Painting by Ayako Ebihara

About the Author

Isao Ebihara, D.Phil. (Oxford Graduate School, TN), a native of Japan, has resided in Canada for over 20 years. He has been teaching Japanese language courses at Trinity Western University in British Colombia since the fall of 2002. His academic training encompasses theology, psychology and literature, and his interests include Japanese language, Asian animation and pop culture, culture and spirituality and religions and politics.

In this book, Dr. Ebihara explores the philosophical and religious/spiritual background of the anime authors and stories and a history of their productions. He has a thorough knowledge of Japanese anime culture and recognizes its great impact on the global community.

All The World Is Anime
978-1-935434-05-4

an imprint of
GlobalEd AdvancePress

www.ingramcontent.com/pod-product-compliance
Lightning Source LLC
Chambersburg PA
CBHW061305110426
42742CB00012BA/2061